SELF-ESTEEM:
the magical key to a world of . . .

- successful relationships
- joyous achievement
- inner peace
- powerful independence
- the freedom of self-acceptance

Discover the happiness that can
only be found by . . .
being your own best friend.

BE YOUR OWN
BEST FRIEND

LOUIS PROTO is the author of *Take Charge of Your Life*; *Self-Healing*; *Meditation for Everybody*; *Increase Your Energy*, and a number of other books.

Be Your Own Best Friend

How to Achieve Greater
Self-Esteem, Health, and
Happiness

LOUIS PROTO

BERKLEY BOOKS, NEW YORK

BE YOUR OWN BEST FRIEND

A Berkley Book / published by arrangement with
Piatkus Books

PRINTING HISTORY
Piatkus edition published 1993
Berkley edition / July 1994

All rights reserved.
Copyright © 1993 by Louis Proto.
This book, or parts thereof, may not be reproduced
in any form without permission.
For information address:
The Berkley Publishing Group, a division of Penguin Putnam Inc.,
375 Hudson Street, New York, New York 10014.

The Penguin Putnam Inc. World Wide Web site address is
http://www.penguinputnam.com

ISBN: 0-425-14296-5

BERKLEY®
Berkley Books are published by
The Berkley Publishing Group, a division of Penguin Putnam Inc.,
375 Hudson Street, New York, New York 10014.
BERKLEY and the "B" design are trademarks
belonging to Penguin Putnam Inc.

PRINTED IN THE UNITED STATES OF AMERICA

16   15   14   13   12   11   10   9

Contents

She knew him and flew to him, and embraced him, and held him fast, and called out:

"Kai, dear little Kai! At last I have found you!"

But he sat quite still, stiff and cold. Then little Gerda wept hot tears that fell upon his breast. They penetrated into his heart, they thawed the lump of ice, and consumed the little piece of glass in his eye.

Now he recognized her, and cried rejoicingly:

"Gerda, dear Gerda! Where have you been all this time? And where have I been?"

—*The Snow Queen,* Hans Christian Andersen

Acknowledgments

My thanks are due to the following publishers for permission to quote briefly from their books:

Celestial Arts, Berkeley, California (*Love is Letting Go of Fear* by Gerald G. Jampolsky)
Pan Books, London (*Jonathon Livingston Seagull* by Richard Bach)
Piatkus Books (*Codependency* by David Stafford and Liz Hodgkinson)
Century Hutchinson (*Love, Medicine and Miracles* by Bernie Siegel)

Quotations from the Tao Te Ching are from the translation by Gia-Fu Feng, illustrated by Jane French and published by Wildwood House, London.

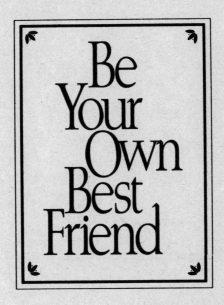

Be
Your
Own
Best
Friend

Teach only Love, for that is what you are
—A Course in Miracles, Helen Schucman

Chapter 1

Loving Yourself:
An Introduction

"HAPPINESS," SAYS LOUISE HAY, A REMARK-
able woman from California who healed herself of
cancer in six months and now teaches her techniques and passes on her philosophy to others, "is
feeling good about yourself. When you *don't* feel good
about yourself, you don't feel good. Period."

To some readers this may be a little startling.
We tend to believe that we would be happy if we
had *more* of what we think we want, for example,
more money, more success, more leisure . . . Yet the
truth is that these things do not really satisfy our
most basic need which is to feel loved, and loved
unconditionally for who we are. What we really need
in order to be happy with ourselves is to feel that we
have a right to be here, alive on this planet and that,
in spite of any faults we may have, we are OK, or at
least as OK as anybody else.

As well as making us feel good, a healthy self-image makes life a whole lot easier. We have more confidence and humor, are more relaxed, and therefore enjoy social interaction more than if we are timid, tense or depressed. If we respect ourselves, others will respond by according respect to us. We will get the jobs we want, because we present ourselves to prospective employers as capable, as winners rather than losers. In our intimate relationships, to the extent that we are in touch with our own power, we will not have to try to feel secure by draining our partner's energy, by manipulating, guilt-slinging, blaming and complaining. We will be more interested in *playing with* them rather than in struggling for dominance over them—which makes us more fun to be with. And, if you know and accept who you are, you will not be frightened of intimacy or commitment.

If you love yourself, it shows: in your facial expression, your bearing and your body-language, and the things you say about yourself . . . You will know that you have as much right as anybody else to take your place in the world and will take your space accordingly. You will take the trouble to groom yourself, to look after your health and generally to be kind to your body. In Chapter 5 we shall see that how we feel about ourselves is closely linked with what happens in our bodies, for better or for worse.

"No man is an island . . ."

We tend to treat other people in the same way as we treat ourselves, and other people tend to treat us according to the silent clues we are giving them about how *we* expect to be treated. If you are constantly subliminally broadcasting by your body language and by what you say that you are no good, an inadequate human being or a victim, you are actually inviting others to victimize you. There can be no persecutors without those willing to offer themselves as victims.

Similarly, if you are accustomed to treating yourself harshly, you will tend to be hard on others. If you cannot trust yourself, how can you trust other people? Or how can you forgive them if you do not have it in your heart to forgive yourself? The language of trust and forgiveness will be unfamiliar territory and alien to you. It works both ways. The type of energy we are putting out into the world is the kind of energy we get back—multiplied. "Judge not, lest ye be judged" is simply the way it is, the way energy works. Every judgment we make about others in fact tells us more about ourselves than about them: our boundaries, self-limitations and the things we cannot give ourselves permission to be . . .

Feeling good about yourself makes you more spontaneous, more authentic. You don't have to keep a tight rein on yourself, continually censoring what you say in case you give away how you really are inside. You can give yourself permission to express yourself freely. For the self-lover there are no "shoulds", only self-expression. You will not feel that you have to placate everybody, to bend over backwards trying to win their approval. If you are more tolerant of criticism, taking yourself less seriously, you will be less paranoid, less thin-skinned and less easily upset by what others think of you.

And remember that you cannot please other people all the time. That is not what you are here for. You are here to sing your own song, to be who you are—and to enjoy it. And in any case, if you are not being authentic, how can you ever really know that any love that comes your way is really for *you* and not for the false self you are so desperately presenting? It is better to please yourself for a change, by being your own best friend, and allowing the spontaneous Child who is deep within you to come out and play in all its freshness and innocence (see Chapter 4).

A low self-image is behind much of the malaise that affects the quality of many people's lives in all departments, from physical and mental health to relationships and performance at work. This low self-image may account for:

- shyness and lack of confidence;
- inability to stand up for ourselves;
- underachievement, inhibition of creativity;
- excessive desire to please others;
- poverty consciousness;
- fear of intimacy;
- inability to receive from others;
- excessive dependence, jealousy and possessiveness;
- addictions (e.g. to alcohol, drugs, promiscuity, overeating);
- paranoia, oversensitivity to criticism and projection of our own negativity on to others;
- need to control to feel safe;

- self-destructive behavior, accident-proneness (and if self-hatred is extreme, even suicide);
- victim consciousness (manifested in envy, blaming, manipulating, harboring resentments);
- inability to enjoy and express ourselves, to experience freedom and joy.

On the other hand, if you feel *good* about yourself you will radiate a more positive, powerful image. Signs of a healthy self-image include:

- confidence and optimism;
- clarity as to what we want—and trust that we can get it without damaging others;
- absence of guilt and self-recrimination;
- ability to love and to forgive;
- capacity to tolerate intimacy;
- maintaining a sense of self in relationships;
- having preferences rather than addictions;
- freedom of self-expression;
- ability to enjoy;
- prosperity consciousness;
- non-seriousness;
- ability to say "No".

In this book you will learn how to improve your self-image and to love yourself, *for who you are,* so that you will be able to be your own best friend. Once you can do this you will be well on the way to achieving happiness.

A merry heart doeth good like a medicine
—Proverbs, 16.22

Chapter 2

How High Is Your Self-Esteem?

THE FIRST STEP ON THE ROAD TO LOVING yourself more is to think about your sense of self-esteem, and then to set about doing something to make it higher.

To help you assess how healthy your self-image is, try answering the following twenty questions.

1. Are you able to say "No"—and mean it?

2. What sort of people do you envy, and why?

3. How do you feel about your body?

4. How would you rate your looks:
    a) dazzling?

b) fair?
c) plain?
d) ugly?

5. Do you feel there a) is, or b) has been, enough love in your life?

6. When somebody gives you a present you didn't expect do you say:
    a) "You shouldn't have!"
    b) "What have I done to deserve this?"
    c) "Thank you?"

7. What do you feel when you are paid a glowing compliment:
    a) surprise?
    b) disbelief?
    c) pleased?

8. Do you feel that you are sufficiently appreciated, both at work and at home?

9. When buying new clothes for yourself do you go for:
    a) quality?
    b) price?

10. When was the last time you allowed yourself to be extravagant?

11. Do you think that you deserve the best?

_____

12. How do you handle your anger? Do you:
     a) pretend everything is all right?
     b) feel guilty about being angry?
     c) sulk?

_____

13. Are you able to "take your space" whenever
     you need to without feeling guilty?

_____

14. Do you experience intimacy with the right
     person as:
     a) satisfying
     b) scary

_____

15. Are you accident prone?

_____

16. What sort of people make you feel uncomfort-
     able?

_____

17. Do you feel guilty if you don't meet others' ex-
     pectations of you?

_____

18. Do you always feel that you don't have enough
     money?

_____

19. Would you say that you are critical of yourself?

_____

20. Do you have a constant source of worry or anxiety?

_____

By now, you may well be wondering what these questions have in common, and what they have to do with the way you see yourself. What, for example, is the connection between being accident-prone and always being short of money? Or envying other people with not being able to handle your anger?

But in fact, _everything_ that happens to us is directly connected to the way we see ourselves, because our self-image (healthy or otherwise) is like a filter through which we interpret our experiences. Life reflects _us_, and we get the sort of experiences, deep down, that we think we deserve. Quite simply, we make our experiences happen, albeit unconsciously.

Accident-proneness is a good example of this. It is very much associated with a sense of guilt, perhaps stemming from way back in our childhood and the hidden need for expiation of that guilt, for punishment. Some people cannot seem to work in the kitchen, for example, without disasters occurring: either they will scald themselves in hot water, or cut a finger while chopping onions. Of course this could happen to anyone. But if it happens regularly one must begin to suspect a pattern—a recurring habitual phenomenon—that goes beyond mere clumsiness. You cannot love yourself if you really hate yourself deep down.

Self-destructive patterns

This deep-seated sense of guilt and need for punishment can spill out in other ways, too. There is little difference between, for example, sexual and spiritual masochism. The hair shirt and the self-flagellation of penitents, it could be said, are as satisfying at some very deep level as acting out the role of victim in sexual terms.

These may be extreme examples, but they do occur. More common is the way a self-hater seems to try to sabotage deliberately any good experiences he or she might otherwise have had. It is as if one part of them sets up a pleasurable experience, and another part (the one that feels they don't deserve to have a good time) manages somehow to ruin it. Things are always "going wrong" for them, and they never seem able to take responsibility for themselves.

You may be able to recognize such people (perhaps yourself?) by their excessive use of such phrases as:

"With my luck I'm not surprised . . ."
"Nobody gives you anything in this life . . ."
"If you'd had the setbacks I've had . . ."
"Not again! . . ."

Phrases like these are part of the vocabulary of the victim.

I know a woman, Sheila, who always seems to have bad experiences whenever she goes away on holiday. One year Sheila lost her passport, another year her currency and travelers' checks. She is resigned to being confined to her hotel room regularly with "Mediterranean tummy" and puts it all

down to "just her luck." When Sheila came for counselling her "presenting problem" (i.e. her reason for
seeking therapy) had apparently nothing at all to
do with her low self-image. Her problem was that
she was desperately unhappy after the break-up of
a relationship that had lasted for several years. As
we explored her feelings together she came up with
the grief and the anger that usually accompanies a
loss of this kind. But the feeling that was the most
painful of all was regret that it was somehow her
fault that she had lost the man she loved. "If only
I hadn't . . . ," "If only I had . . . ," "I should have
been more . . ." were the thoughts with which she
tortured herself.

Core complexes

When one goes deep enough into the unconscious
parts of the personality (whether through therapy
or simple introspection), one eventually uncovers
the basic "core" complex which lies behind seem-
ingly unconnected ways of being and experiencing.
It did not surprise me that Sheila had such "bad
luck" with her holidays, or that her relationship had
ended in the way it did. For these occurrences were
manifestations of her basic lack of self-esteem. She
simply did not feel (unconsciously of course) that
she deserved to be happy, to have a good time and
the best of everything. She did not allow love to
reach her. She didn't trust it.

Sheila had a constant need for reassurance from
her lover that drove him to distraction to the extent
that he decided to move out. She had become cling-
ing and compliant, which made her boring, and she

had lost all sense of being her own person. Naturally, when the relationship folded it was catastrophic for her. She felt that she had lost a part of herself. The truth of the matter was that she had given it away because she did not value it.

It took many more therapy sessions before Sheila was willing to accept that her partner had not left her because she was a "Bad Person," but because it was his choice to move on, and to forgive him for "doing his own thing." Eventually she even progressed in her self-validation to the point where she could say, albeit wryly, "Well, that was *his* loss. *I'm* OK." She could well have added, in the words of the Sondheim song, "And I'm still here."

Until our "core" complexes are brought into our awareness we will be at their mercy. We will go on repeating the same self-limiting and self-destructive patterns, year in, year out. We can change our partners, but will go on having the same sort of relationships and playing the same desperate games. For unless we change ourselves, nothing really changes.

And the way we see ourselves is the most crucial "core" complex of the lot as far as the quality we experience in our lives is concerned. In my score or so years of working with people I have found that, more often than not, it is the "bottom line." And I suspect that it is introjection by the client of the therapist's "unconditional positive regard" that, more than any other factor, allows the healing of our emotional wounds to happen. In Chapter 5 we will be seeing how love and loving ourselves can heal, not only emotionally, but physically as well.

If we do not love ourselves enough (and most of us don't, if we are honest or aware enough to admit it) it feels as if we have a "black hole" inside us. We feel empty, hollow. We become easy prey to anxiety and depression, which can drive some people to the point of suicide when they feel they can take no more. And what is suicide but passing the ultimate sentence of punishment upon oneself? Hopefully, it doesn't go this far.

Addictions

There are other ways to be self-destructive, and addictions are a good example. Whether the addiction is to alcohol, drugs, food or relationships does not make much difference. The important point is that addicts, of whatever sort, are trying to make themselves feel better than they do, to fill their "black hole" and make life seem, even though temporarily, worth living again.

Addictive behaviors are behaviors that are out of control, leading to negative consequences, but are persisted in anyway. We usually indulge in them to get high or get numb.

Another client of mine used to ward off anxiety by over-eating. Even after going out to dinner with friends, Joan would feel impelled to raid the fridge when she returned home and devour anything she could find there. Her pathology was that she hated her body. Predictably, her sex life was a disaster area. Her convent education (or at least, what she made of it) had left her totally out of touch with her instinctual energy. As she put on more weight she viewed her body (when she could bear to look at it) with increasing distaste. She could never persevere with a diet, which made her feel even more inadequate. She was also very lonely, and aware that she wasn't getting any younger.

Attempts like this to fill an inner spiritual void with *things* just do not work. The gnawing emptiness remains, or at least, it quickly returns. There is no substitute for love, and especially for loving ourselves unconditionally.

Conditioning

We may well ask, why is it so rare to find somebody who loves himself or herself unconditionally? The answer is simply that we have never been taught to do this. Unless we have been very fortunate in our upbringing, any approval that has come our way has been conditional: in other words on meeting the expectations of others (especially our parents and teachers). We have been conditioned to "behave ourselves," to do "the right thing." Undoubtedly, these significant adults in our lives acted with the best intentions.

And it is true that many of the things they taught us were necessary for us to learn in the interests of survival and social adaptation, e.g. looking both ways before we crossed the road, being polite to others and so forth. But, too often, over the years we got the message that pleasing other people and meeting their expectations were ends in themselves. We have not been taught to please ourselves without incurring the accusation of selfishness. Pleasing ourselves could too often result in punishment or, at least, loss of love. And so most of us conformed. The rebels among us were more often than not reacting against authority rather than choosing self-expression.

Guilt

Much religious teaching, imperfectly understood or taught in a half-baked fashion, fosters guilt, perfectionism and the denial of our "lower nature" (which usually means our sexuality). Paranoia about our sins (usually the fun things of life) and Divine Retribution figure prominently in fundamentalist Christianity. It is almost as if we were born *bad* and have to make up for it by wading through this "vale of tears," rather like Alice in Wonderland when she too was depressed about her situation. Enjoying ourselves "for the hell of it" seems to be just asking for trouble from the Judge who sees and hears all, rather like an archetypal Peeping Tom in the sky.

A misunderstanding of the doctrine of penance and the need to purify ourselves constantly through prayer can lead to the elevation of suffering into a virtue *per se*. If we suffer enough in this life presumably we shall eventually be able to slither back into the Garden of Eden, from which our First Parents were expelled for trying to be too clever and rising above their station.

This is not to deny the undoubted comfort, inspiration and support which are available in religious precepts that are positive and life-affirming. Too often, however, we forget that the heart of Christianity is love or, as Saint Paul put it, "charity." And charity begins at home, in other words, with ourselves. Far from being an impiety, to love ourselves is what we have been specifically commanded to do in the New Testament. It bears repeating: "*Love thy neighbor as thyself.*" And understandably, only if you can love yourself "warts and all," does love of your neighbor become possible in spite of *his* warts.

And yet, curiously, to think highly of ourselves (or, if we do, to admit it) is not something we can do without incurring a charge of being egotistical, "self-centered" or "pushy." Some cultures (particularly the British) seem to have elevated self-deprecation into a positive virtue!

Even if you secretly *do* feel you are OK, conditioning says you must pretend to be modest and underplay your achievements. Certainly you must not shout from the housetops "I'm great!" or feel that you are special in any way. This is a pity, because you *are*. We all are. We are all magnificent, amazing originals. But then, this is only to be expected, since we were all fashioned in the image of God. Either we are *all* special—or nobody is.

How can we love ourselves more?

In the chapters that follow, we will explore the answers to this question in greater detail, but for now I want to give you a list of helpful pointers.

We can learn to love ourselves more in the following ways.

1. By constant vigilance as to when we are blaming ourselves, feeling guilty, or otherwise "putting ourselves down" in our heads.

2. By reversing our conditioned negative attitudes through making positive statements to ourselves. The mind is a computer and has to be reprogrammed. This we can do by affirmations and visualizations (examples are given throughout the book). If this is done on a daily basis, the way we see ourselves starts to change. Since our feelings and actions all stem from thoughts, if we think positively we start to feel better about ourselves and to act accordingly.

3. By actualizing our new insights, i.e. acting "as if" we are already the way we want to be. And you can be any way you like.

4. By never allowing any invalidation of ourselves (whether from within or without) to pass unchallenged.

5. By treating ourselves as well as we have been taught to treat other people.

6. By presenting ourselves in the world as if we deserve respect for who we are and the best of everything (which is in fact the case), and by giving ourselves permission to enjoy. And by coming from a place of Abundance rather than Poverty. Others will respond to us according to our energy vibrations. We create our own reality according to our thoughts.

7. By an ongoing, non-judgmental openness to discover who we really are through self-enquiry (e.g. meditation, therapy, prayer, dreams, interaction with others), and always with *total forgiveness of our "mistakes."*

After a time, Fletcher Gull dragged himself into the sky and faced a brand-new group of students, eager for their first lesson. "To begin with," he said heavily, "you've got to understand that a seagull is an unlimited idea of freedom, an image of the Great Gull, and your whole body, from wingtip to wingtip, is nothing more than your thought itself." —Jonathon Livingston Seagull, Richard Bach

Chapter 3

Changing Your Mind

WHAT WE TELL OURSELVES, THE INFORMA-
tion and thoughts that fill our minds, is supremely
important if we are going to be able to love ourselves
and to become our own best friend. What we must
do, as Johnny Mercer sang, is "Accentuate the positive, eliminate the negative" in order to create our
future by what we think, say and feel now.

The power of ideas

The reality we experience is the sum total of our
thoughts. The meanings we give to events, the conclusions we draw about "the way it is," the image
we have about ourselves, and the past we create
and the future we imagine become our reality, or the
filter in our minds through which we interpret outer
reality. Therefore, what we tell ourselves *inwardly*

is supremely important. If we are constantly judging ourselves in our heads, telling ourselves that we shouldn't have done this or can't do that, we limit ourselves. Words like "should" and "can't" castrate our positive energy. If we are continually putting ourselves down (or, indeed, allowing put-downs from others to go unchallenged), we are very likely to *feel* down and depressed about ourselves, and fuel our negative thoughts more and more.

Words are immensely powerful. Think how whole nations can be swayed by propaganda. If ideas are repeated often enough, they soon get taken for granted as the truth. Warlike or racist slogans can even generate a murderous frenzy and lead to hell on earth. Just think of Nazi Germany. Similarly, on an individual level, we feel and act in accordance with what we think to be true. Thoughts give rise to feelings, which are then acted out. If we tell ourselves that we *can't* swim, are *no good* at saying "no" and *should* complain about that bad meal but probably won't, there's a pretty good chance that you are telling yourself the truth! Replace the negative words with positive ones and you are already one step on the way to feeling confident about your ability and to go about acting it out.

Everything that is, started life as a thought. Thoughts are like seeds which, if we give them energy by cultivating them, will take root and eventually bear fruit. We give them energy by feeding them with attention, for attention *is* energy. Consider for a moment how everything that has been created on the material plane started as an idea, a project, in somebody's mind. Whether it was a painting, a building or a piece of furniture, the process was the same. The artist, architect or craftsperson *actualized* an idea in which he or she believed by feeding it energy and by working on it. What was at first just a thought, invisible and tenuous, became manifested on the material plane, solid, tangible and very "real."

This is what happens with our minds. The things that manifest in our lives, for better or for worse, are the results of our thoughts. They can thus be said to be our own creations. This applies equally to what we become.

Life is a mirror

What usually happens, however, is that we feel a lot of the things that happen to us really have nothing to do with us, as in the case of the woman whose holidays always turned into bad luck stories. But life is, in fact, always mirroring *us*. It unerringly reflects back to us where we are at. If we are positive and caring, we will be surrounded by positive, caring people. The reverse is also unfortunately true: being negative is to attract negative experiences. This wisdom is expressed in sayings like "Everybody loves a lover" and "Cry and you cry alone." You don't have to believe in this. Try it out for yourself and see whether or not it is true for you. Do a little experiment. See if you can trace any connection between the events you experience during one normal day, both bad and good, and your state of mind at the time. Can you draw any conclusions from this?

"Your environment is only as high as you are" says the *Lazy Man's Guide to Enlightenment*. If this seems weird to you that is not surprising. For most people the commonsense thing to do if there is something upsetting you in your surroundings is to try and change it. We lose sight of the fact that, yes, this is happening, but our reaction to it is *our* reaction, and our feelings about it are *our* feelings. We rarely stop to consider what we ourselves contributed to what happened, not least by our thoughts and expectations, or ask ourselves just *why* this incident, or this person, upsets us so much.

Change the inner, the outer follows

You are the center of the universe that you are creating with your thoughts from moment to moment. If you don't like your creation, choose to change it by working on it from the inside out. Changing our attitudes, choosing to see things in a different light and to put out a different energy is the way transformation of our reality happens, in life as in therapy.

Sometimes it can be hard, if you are convinced you are right and that "this is the way it is." But remember that things always look "the way they are" from the standpoint you are taking. It couldn't be any other way. In this sense, everyone is "right all the time." But Helen Schucman in her *Course in Miracles* asks, "Would you rather be healthy and happy, or do you want to be right?" Being "right" is the booby prize if it involves stress, confrontation, anxiety and resentment. Peace of mind and the best quality of life we can create for ourselves, is really what everybody wants. But we have to be prepared to work for them and to make them top priorities.

And creating what we want is not as hard as it sounds. Really, it is just a matter of being willing to give up old patterns and to change our ideas about "who we are" and "how it is." The problem (if there is one) is that we have lived with these ideas and habits of behavior for so long that we have become identified with them. For Gurdjieff (an early 20th-century esoteric thinker, healer and teacher, who believed his philosophy could be absorbed by discipline and self-observation), this identification with old habits is the "only sin," in the sense that it blinds us to new possibilities and ways of being, and carries its own built-in pain. And hang on to old ideas we do, as if our life depended on them. We feel threatened whenever they are challenged and defend them tooth and nail.

It has been said that a sign of madness is not *what* we believe, but how addicted to believing it we are. Some people are so destroyed by the collapse of their cherished beliefs, that they have been known to destroy themselves as a result. They do not see how they can go on living without the "props" which have made life meaningful for them.

We are not our *ideas*. Our belief systems should support *us*, not the other way round. They are "movable feasts," and we must be prepared to change them when they no longer serve and support us. *We can be any way we want to be*. We don't have to be stuck with feeling bad about ourselves—unless, of course, we are addicted to being a martyr or a victim. We can *choose* what to think and feel about the way we are. And anyway, all interpretations are relative. Who's to say we are wrong about ourselves?

The remarkable thing is that, however we choose to see ourselves, we will continually find evidence in our environment to prove that we are right, that this is in fact the way we truly are. This is not surprising, for we will be continually *looking for* evidence of how awful we are, and will effectively block out of our awareness all evidence to the contrary that comes our way. If we do not love ourselves, no love can reach us—not because we are unlovable, but because we will not let it in. We probably won't even notice it, because we are simply not geared to see it.

Affirmations

What we tell ourselves is supremely important, and one of the best ways to improve our self-image is to tell ourselves *repeatedly* that we are OK. In other words, we need to be our own best friend. We have to stop this sadistic internal dialogue with ourselves in which we always come out *wrong*, and replace it with affirmative, positive and validating statements that will eventually sink into our unconscious and reprogram the computers that are our minds. These life-affirming statements are called "affirmations."

You do not even have to believe these affirmations for them to work, although it certainly helps. All you are doing is reprogramming your mind with positive pictures, knowing that all of us react to what we *think* is true. We cannot see any difference between "real" and "imagined" reality, as the Japanese schoolchildren, reported in the *Kyushi Journal of Medical Science* (1962), demonstrated when they manifested an allergic reaction to being brushed with harmless plants after being told they were, in fact, poison ivy. As Shakespeare said (*Hamlet*, II. ii), "There is nothing either good or bad, but thinking makes it so."

The best-known affirmation is: "Every day, in every way, I am getting better and better." It was used by Emil Coué with the patients at his clinic in Nancy, northern France, about seventy years ago, with such spectacular success that it attracted much publicity. Coué chose this particular affirmation because it was non-specific, and would therefore cover anything that could possibly be wrong with his patients. But affirmations can also be worded to cancel out any more specific area of negativity we may have. Examples of affirmations are given at the end of this chapter and throughout the book. Choose the ones that fit you, and feel free to adapt and modify them to fit your own special needs.

All that you need to make affirmations work for you are *faith* and, especially, *perseverance*. Believe that these words carry the power to change your life, and they will. Persevere in repeating them to yourself, day in, day out, and sooner or later you will begin to experience transformation. Small miracles will start happening in your life as your new positive attitudes start to attract positive experiences.

The best time to practice affirmations is when you are relaxed and do not have a lot of thoughts and internal "Chatter" competing with them. (For more on deep relaxation, see Chapter 8.) Immediately on waking in the morning is a good time, as is just before you drop off to sleep at night. But you can also make affirmations at any time during the day. Take a few deep breaths first to relax your body and assume a comfortable position. Repeat the affirmation you have chosen several times, slowly, and with total conviction. You will know when to stop when the energy starts to go out of it.

Make it a discipline to cancel out any negative thoughts you may have about yourself with a contrary affirmation. Do this whenever you catch yourself in the act of putting yourself down. (This applies, too, to any disparaging remarks other people may make about the way you are, or anything that you feel is an invalidation of you. We will discuss this in more detail in another chapter.)

Here are some affirmations to start you off. They are deliberately very general. You will find more specific affirmations at the end of each chapter, based on the material covered in those chapters. You should also be able to add affirmations of your own.

Here are a few hints on affirmation techniques.

1. Affirmations should be short and tackle single statements at a time.

2. They should always state the positive, rather than deny the negative, i.e. "I approve of myself all the time," rather than "I'm not as bad as I think I am."

3. They should also be set in the present, as if what you want to happen is already the case.

4. They should be repeated twice, allowing time for each statement to sink in.

5. The more relaxed you are, the deeper affirmations will sink into your subconscious.

Examples of affirmations
My thoughts create a world in which I feel safe, healthy, happy and loved.

I love and approve of myself at all times.

I value who I am and what I have to give—and so do others.

Life is good, and gets better every day.

All is well in my wonderful, healthy, peaceful, loving, prosperous, joyful and creative world.

Being happy, successful, prosperous and loved feels totally SAFE.

I deserve the best of everything, simply for who I am.

Everything I touch is a success.

I feel safe with everybody, and at all times.

I am an attractive, successful, intuitive, loving and creative human being.

I win all the time.

I feel gratitude for my life and my many blessings.

Everything I need comes to me easily.

I always get enough. I am enough.

There is no limit to how good I can feel.

I am free to live my life as I choose.

God wants me to be happy.

Visualizations

Another technique you can use to bring about change in your attitudes and feelings about yourself is visualization. To visualize is to use your imagination creatively, and what you create through visualization is another reality to the one you feel stuck with and which is not delivering the goods in making you feel better than you do. You will find examples of visualizations throughout the book, especially where we are looking at the power of love in healing.

Just as affirmations are based on the power of words to influence our unconscious, so visualization is based on the power of *images* that we deliberately conjure up in our minds' eye. For example, biofeedback training, which uses sensitive machines to monitor and gain control over automatic, reflex-regulated body functions, has shown how affected we are, both as regards our moods and our physiological processes, by fleeting thoughts and mental images. It is as if our minds can make no difference between what is actually happening "out there" (i.e. in the material world) and what is happening inside our heads. The effect on us will therefore be the same. We will be moved, exalted, depressed, joyful or worried, depending on what we dwell on. Take, for example, films. Really, these are just moving images on a screen. They have no substance in reality. Yet they have the power to make us feel romantic, scared, sexually aroused and so forth.

We tend to become like and move towards the pictures that we carry in our minds. It is thus very important for our well-being that we dwell only on positive images. It is not exaggerating to say that one can make oneself seriously ill, for example, by dwelling on illness. The opposite is equally true, of course. Well-documented "miraculous" cures of cancer have occurred, for example, in patients for whom doctors could do no more but who practised regular visualization.

The techniques for visualization are basically the same as for affirmations.

1. **Relax**. First you need to relax and slow down your thought processes, and to make yourself

comfortable. Making your breathing slower and deeper usually helps, as does becoming aware of how you feel in your body. Give attention to your body sensations. Which muscles, for example, feel tense? Allow them to relax. Let go of any problems that may have been on your mind. Give yourself permission to be at peace for these few moments.

2. **Feel safe**. To assist this winding-down process always start a visualization by conjuring up in your mind a picture of a place where you feel totally safe, and preferably in natural surroundings. It could be a deserted beach, or a beautiful garden, or a special place in the woods, either a place that you have known and enjoyed, or an imaginary one. Spending a few blissful moments in the idyllic spot of your choice.

3. **Create pictures**. Start to create with your thoughts the mental picture that you have already decided is to be the subject of your visualization. Examples are given below, but remember to make the visualization as detailed as you can. Most important of all, get the feeling in your body that what you are visualizing is *actually happening*. If you have difficulty in creating visual images, this does not matter, as long as you can summon up this feeling in your body.

4. **How to stop**. You will know when to stop when the energy starts to go out of your visualization. When you feel that you are finished, let go of

your mental pictures. Put them into a balloon and watch it as it floats off into the sky until you can see it no longer. Afterwards, try to keep the feelings of relaxation as long as you can by taking things easy for as long as possible.

Chapter 4

Self-Acceptance

AS WE SAW IN CHAPTER 2, ONE OF THE BEST
ways of loving ourselves is by forgiving ourselves.
Not once, but over and over again. The same, of
course, applies to forgiving others. Indeed, the way
we treat others is usually the way we treat ourselves. Our relationships are mirrors, and every
judgment we make of others limits us. What we
are in fact saying, whenever we judge others, is
"I cannot allow myself to be or to behave in this
way," thereby constricting our freedom to be any
way we want to be.

Personal growth, loving ourselves, is very much
about learning to accept ourselves, *as we are*. And
if there are parts of ourselves that we find hard to
accept, be sure that they are not likely to disappear
until we *do* learn to accept them. The way out is,
as always, the way *through*. These "rogue" parts of

ourselves have to be accepted as being as much a part of us as the "good" parts of our personalities that we have no difficulty in owning up to. We have to reclaim our "bad" aspects from the limbo to which we have consigned them.

In that limbo, rejected parts of ourselves remain unchanged. Not only do they not disappear of their own accord, but they also take up some of our psychic energy, energy that would otherwise be available to us for living fully. They *suck*, like leeches. They make us feel unworthy, or guilty, or vulnerable. The more we try to sweep them under the carpet of unconsciousness, the more powerful they become until they threaten to control our lives. And repression only makes them stronger. They will haunt us, both in real life and in our dreams, for whatever we dream of is but a part of ourselves which we really want to be acknowledged into consciousness.

Integrating the "Shadow"

Jung gave the name the "Shadow" to these disowned parts of ourselves, and Jungian analysis is largely about becoming aware of how much we are influenced by our "Shadows." Until the shadow is brought into the light of consciousness no real growth is possible. Or peace of mind. The shadow can haunt our dreams, knocking on the door of our psyches, wanting to be admitted to our family of inner selves. Sometimes, if it is very highly charged with energy, it can be the stuff of nightmares, appearing to us as monsters, fierce animals or threatening people pursuing us.

Try as we might, we cannot escape from them.

Literature is full of examples of the power of these disowned parts of ourselves. Caliban in *The Tempest* is Prospero's shadow, as Mr Hyde is Dr Jekyll's, and the picture is Dorian Gray's.

To face our own demons takes courage. It can be a painful process, in which our cherished illusions about ourselves are shattered. Yet, if we really want to know who we are, rather than what we would like to be, the final result of such searching is a sense of integration, a restoration to wholeness. One feels humbled, but also more *real* as the false self crumbles.

Equally important, reclaiming our shadows means that we stop projecting them outwards, on to others, on to the world. For, whatever psychic energies we repress in ourselves, we will also see "out there"— and go on meeting them over and over again. Indeed, we will attract them. Only when they are accepted as part of us, can we stop scapegoating, seeing evil everywhere, being paranoid and persecutory—*and* harshly judgmental. For, remember, what we *see* is always but ourselves, writ large.

Transformation of the energy carried by the Shadow is the stuff of myths and fairy tales, as well as dreams. The alchemists' search for the "philosophers' stone" that could turn base metals into gold, the parable of the prodigal son, the transformation into a prince of the frog kissed by the princess— all these stories are about the reclaiming of the Shadow. The miracle is, that when we can bring ourselves to love the things in us that seem to be totally unlovable, they change and transform themselves into things which hold value for us. Our anger, for example, which could be symbolized in a dream as a roaring lion about to devour us, becomes, when tamed by being willing to enter into dialogue with it, our strength and ability to defend ourselves, a feature we all need to have in our repertoire. It is only because we have been refusing to acknowledge our strength that it has turned against us and become a Shadow.

The transformation of these Calibans through love and acceptance of ourselves is tremendously important for clarity, both as regards our inner life and our relationships to others. "Why beholdest thou the mote that is in thy brother's eye, but considerest not the beam that is in thine own eye?" (Matthew, 7.3). And, you can be sure, if you do not acknowledge your own Shadow, you will find yourself continually meeting Calibans everywhere because you will attract them to you.

Subpersonalities

Our Shadow is not the only part of us that can turn rogue if we are not aware of it. We all have many other "selves," from the "Inner Child" to the "Driver" that it behoves us to become aware of if they are not to control us, our feelings and our actions. These parts are often referred to in psychotherapy as "subpersonalities." This is a good name for them, because they behave like different people inside us. Of course, they aren't. In fact, they are different types of energy. But they are *fixed* patterns of energy, habits of reacting and they are automatic. We all have them, and they make us who we are. Some of them we are aware of, some not. We may be aware, for example, that we are compulsive workers, unable to switch off. Or that we are gamblers who do not know when to stop. Working hard is fine, enjoying the odd "flutter" is fine. The point is, do we have any choice, or are we driven? If the answer is the latter, then of course we are being controlled by the worker or the gambler in us. And, as with all addictions (for this is, in fact, what they are), mere strength of will is not enough to free us from them.

The only way to get rid of something in ourselves that bothers us, that we would rather not be, is to get to know it intimately, to try and understand why it is there, what needs in us it serves, and therefore why we feel we need to hang on to it. All of our subpersonalities developed because in some way they served us and helped us to survive. We do not need to try and annihilate them—which we can't anyway—but only to control them so they do not "pull our strings" any more, i.e, to make us do things that the rest of our "selves" do not want to do. The more we know what our subpersonalities are and how they behave, the more in charge of our lives we become. For we then have more *choice* as to how to act, and we will be able to act less automatically, driven by habit and impulse. Let us get to know some of the main subpersonalities we all have.

The Inner Child
This is the part of us that is innocent, vulnerable, trusting, fresh, capable of intimacy and warmth,

spontaneity and love. It is our capacity to go on learning, to experience a sense of wonder and to be playful. It is the soft center in each of us, our most intimate and sensitive core, the part of us that *feels*. The Inner Child remains with us all our lives, but it is very common for people (especially men) to hide it from the outer world precisely because it is so vulnerable and easily hurt. If we ignore our Inner Child it will start acting up, blaming, fearing, crying for attention, defeating us until we listen.

The Inner Child is not wise in the ways of the world. It wants, above all, to feel safe, loved, held. When this is not forthcoming it is the part of us that feels panic, or loneliness, lost or confused.

It is very important to learn to recognize and nourish your Inner Child, and to listen to what it needs. Unfortunately, the Child is not very good at articulating its needs, just like real children who sometimes drive their parents to distraction by their constant crying and clamoring for attention. But when the child feels good again, *we* feel good, happy, playful, secure.

The Inner Parent/Controller

Because the Inner Child is so vulnerable and not good at coping with the world, we have all developed more or less powerful Inner Parents to protect it. This subpersonality is the introjection of all the authority figures who have ever influenced us in the past: parents, teachers, clergy. We carry them around with us, warning, guiding, controlling in the interests of keeping us safe from harm. It is, for example, our Inner Parent who makes us look both ways before crossing a busy street, or reminds us to dry our hair properly after we have washed it, just like a real parent. Our Inner Parent is also known as the Controller, and we need it to survive.

A problem arises if our Controller is *too* controlling. If we have been over-protected in our childhood, brought up to follow strict religious precepts or punished for minor infringements, we are likely to have developed Controllers that see the world as a dangerous place, and inhibit us from expressing ourselves freely in it. We can develop rigid, perhaps even schizoid personalities. Certainly we will not feel free, or in touch with our own power to be who we want to be and to do what we feel like doing. On the contrary, we will narrow down the way we are in the world to conform to what was expected of us by those who brought us up. We are still trying to please Mummy, Daddy and our teachers, even though they may no longer be with us. And if we don't, we are likely to feel paranoia and guilt, and even a Bad Person. The Controller is the most upright of our personalities.

We must learn to recognize when we are controlling too much and that the best way to handle our Controller is to deal with the feelings underlying our need to control. These feelings may well include fear in some form.

The Pleaser

As well as feeling that we have to please our Inner Parent in order to feel OK, we have all learned, in the past, to please others in order to feel loved. This is a full-time job sometimes if our need for others' approval is very important to us. The need to meet the expectations of early authority figures is carried over into adult life. We bend over backwards trying to meet the expectations of our girl-friends, boy-friends, peer group, spouses and employers. In our desperation to be popular and accepted we sell ourselves short and drain our energy. We don't say "No" when we need to, accept commitments we would be better off without, are crushed by criticism and unable to defend ourselves if attacked. For the Pleaser, being *liked* is the most important thing in the world.

Many people who are manipulated by their Pleasers are actually storing up a lot of anger, because they are not able to be straight with others and feel frustrated at not being able to ask for what they want.

We must learn to please ourselves before trying to please other people, and in order to do this we need to trust ourselves to behave in a loving, nurturing way because we love others, not to make them love us.

Codependents are archetypal Pleasers, always putting others before themselves and depending on them for their self-esteem. This is self-destructive and even manipulative behavior, and is an important topic which will be examined in more detail in Chapter 9.

The Critic
This subpersonality works closely with the Inner Parent to keep us on the "straight and narrow." Of all our subpersonalities, this one has the most

power to wreck our peace of mind and make us feel bad about ourselves. It is an inner voice that can be quite sadistic, and never lets up nagging us about our shortcomings. With the Critic, we are always wrong. And, if you are unlucky enough to have ended up with a Perfectionist Critic, there is no way you can ever give yourself credit for anything, feel satisfied with your life, or even feel OK. Your Critic will always be on your back like some vicious harpy, undermining your confidence and zest for living, sometimes even to the point of suicide, which is, after all, the ultimate "thumbs down" about yourself.

Of all our subpersonalities, the Critic is the one to be most aware of, and wary of. The Critic in us can make us miserable and depressed, lose confidence and, ultimately, even drive us mad.

The voice of the Critic is instantly recognizable. It is harsh, judgmental, always telling us what is wrong with us and how we should be. It can be relentless in its demands for "perfection" (whatever that may be).

One way to handle your Critic is keep a list of all the things it tells you you must do. (This is also a good way of handling your Driver/Workaholic subpersonality, see below.) Eventually you will get the message that in no way can you *ever* satisfy your Critic's demands on you (which are really your demands on yourself). You can run yourself into the ground and still these sadistic parts of you will be holding the whip over you, goading you ever onwards. The truth is that the Critic doesn't care about *you*. And it hasn't yet got the message that you are perfect anyway, or at least, perfectly imperfect.

The Driver

The Driver (or Workaholic) is the part of us that impels us to work even when there is no need. Unless we do, the Driver makes us feel restless, unsatisfied. It is the most manic of subpersonalities, and tends to get more out of control the older we get. I know a man who gets up at dawn every day and starts cleaning up his house even before he has breakfast. You have probably met a compulsively ambitious businessperson, or an excessively houseproud woman who snatches your ashtray and washes it as soon as you stub out your cigarette, and who seems always to be in the kitchen mopping up, ironing or cleaning. It is a truism that cleanliness is next to godliness, and when it is "over the top" it can also be very unhealthy. At the very least, an overactive Driver does not enable you or the people you live with to relax. And at worst, it could well give you a coronary.

Loosening your subpersonalities' control

If any of your subpersonalities is out of control the only way to bring them back to heel is to get to understand where their energy is coming from, and to take the reins back into your own hands. Merely telling yourself that you should not be like this will not change anything. Remember that subpersonalities, however inconvenient they may be, are there for a purpose. You developed them to help you to survive (for example, the Controller, the Pleaser) and they will go on trying to "do their thing"—often in conflict with each other—until they feel that they are seen and heard by you. For example, your Inner Child will continue to make you feel anxious and insecure until it feels that you are looking after its needs. The Controller will continue to inhibit you and make you feel uptight, in spite of all your efforts to loosen up and have fun. Your Driver will push you to exhaustion because it wants you to be successful and financially secure.

So how can we get to loosen the control exercised by our subpersonalities over the way we are without suppressing their voices completely and fulfilling the needs they represent? One answer is to enter into dialogue with them and get to know them intimately, why they are there, why they are so strident, and what they want for you and from you.

If you listen to yourself, observe yourself in action, you will soon get to recognize your main subpersonalities. They are many, for "we are verily a crowd." Remember that some manipulate most of us, but some are very specific.

Several techniques of entering into dialogue with the various parts of your personality have been developed in humanistic psychology.

Transactional Analysis (TA)

The best-known technique is Transactional Analysis, probably as a result of two best-selling books about it, *Games People Play* by Eric Berne (founder of TA) and *I'm OK, You're OK* by Thomas A. Harris. TA postulates that at any one time we relate to others from the position of Parent, Adult or Child.

It is only if two people are relating to each other on an Adult level that true communication is possible. If they are both into the Parent part of their personalities they will be only interested in controlling and scoring points off each other. If one or other goes off into the Child there will be much blaming, complaining and, perhaps, tears or tantrums.

Analyzing these "transactions" between people is to clarify the dynamic that is going on between them to find out what they really want from each other. TA is a way of trying to see the *place* from which people are really coming, rather than just taking what they are saying or how they are behaving at face value.

Gestalt Therapy

Gestalt Therapy is one of the modern, meditative approaches to personal growth through knowledge of our subpersonalities. Its founder, Fritz Perls, charted the various layers of personality and conditioning we need to cut through before we can experience being "real" and authentic again. These layers are roughly what happens when we wrestle with the question "Who am I?" The layers range from Level I—the cliché layer, used when we exchange social pleasantries—to Level 5, the explosive layer, where we break through to a level of authentic self-expression.

Perls made his reputation at Esalen (the world's first "growth center" at Big Sur, California), by exteriorizing and stage-managing, with a showman's panache, the inner dog-fight going on all the time between the yea-sayer and the nay-sayer in us all.

Before the fascinated eyes of Gestalt group participants, Perls would have the "top dog" and the "underdog" of a group member confront each other verbally, their host shifting between the two cushions representing the combatants and giving alternately a voice to each. What was so amazing was the *articulateness* of these inner voices, of which the person's Ego had been perhaps unaware until then. Each subpersonality was clear as to what it wanted, would often complain at never having been allowed expression in the person's lifestyle, and would even describe with some glee its stratagems for manipulating its host's Ego to get its needs met, or to sabotage projects which it felt were not in its own interests. By the end of the session, a compromise might have been reached by the polarized subpersonalities (conflict resolution), but if not, at least the person would return to the group with a more Aware Ego.

Gestalt Therapy seeks to bring unconscious motivations to one's awareness. Awareness is, in fact, the beginning and the end of Gestalt, and there is an insistence on staying in the present, and allowing oneself to *feel* what is happening from moment to moment. A Gestalt therapist can pick up confused clues from his or her client, possibly including clues from the client's tone of voice and body posture. The therapist may also ask the confused client what exactly his or her confusion means, how it is serving him or her at this moment, and *how* exactly the client is confusing him or herself. Gestalt Therapy is more interested in "how" we do what we do, than "why," since in fact, we never really know *why* we do anything. It can only be conjecture. On the other hand, if we can become aware of *how* we do things, we are rescued from behaving like robots, automatically and unconsciously, and can recapture our power to do something different next time. In other words we have more choice.

Voice Dialogue

The most sophisticated technique evolved, so far, for getting to know our inner selves (or subpersonalities) better and giving us more choice of how to be, is undoubtedly Voice Dialogue. It has been developed by two Californian therapists, Dr Hal Stone (a former Jungian analyst) and his wife Dr Sidra Winkelman, and is a combination of elements of TA, Gestalt and other techniques, which makes for a deceptively simple tool for enhancing awareness of our subpersonalities.

In a Voice Dialogue training group in London a few years ago Sidra told the group members how they had hit on this very simple but penetrating approach purely by chance. She and Hal were having an argument and engaging in the usual ping-pong; "You did this, you did that" etc. It could have gone on for ever with nothing being resolved as long as they were both entrenched in their respective aggrieved positions of Controlling Parent and Rebellious Daughter (which were the subpersonalities that had taken them over).

Suddenly, Sidra became aware from her experience of working with people as a therapist of the tone of voice of her husband and his body posture. It struck her that he had become very much like a sulky, plaintive child. She therefore abandoned her attempts to be "right" and to defend herself against recrimination, and started to talk to Hal as if he indeed was a hurt Child, and from the space of being Good Mother rather than Rebellious Daughter.

She started to speak to him more gently, to ask what was wrong, and what he needed from her. The effect on Hal was electric. In a small voice, like a little boy, he started to tell her how insecure he felt, both about their relationship and the work he was doing. At that time he was involved in setting up The Center for The Healing Arts in Los Angeles, the first such center to be established in the US. He was experiencing a lot of self-doubt and anxiety about funding, and felt that it was all too much of a responsibility.

It was, in fact, his Inner Child that was feeling vulnerable and unsure, and when Sidra started to address this Child the dynamic between them changed dramatically. She encouraged the Frightened Little Boy to say what he needed to feel less unsafe, reassured him that everything would be all right, and that he could count on her full support. Eventually they stopped talking, and she held him like a baby in her arms.

Hal emerged from this encounter with more awareness of the pressures that he had been putting on himself. He now had the insight into what his Inner Child needed, which he hadn't had before. Just as well, for otherwise, starved of nourishment, his Child might well have made him ill in order to get his needs met. The Child in all of us can be immensely powerful: it is possibly behind much illness, absenteeism and sabotage of our cherished projects if it is not looked after.

From uncovering the existence of the Child, Hal and Sidra became interested in identifying which other subpersonalities were influencing them without their being aware of it. They helped each other become conscious of their Pleasers, Critics and, strong in Hal's case, the Driver. They learned how to bring these dimly-felt troublemakers forwards, to talk to them and ask them what they wanted, and how they felt neglected by the Ego (the collective sum of our subpersonalities), and what would make them behave in harmony rather than causing problems.

One thing they discovered was that subpersonalities would only come out and engage in dialogue if they felt acceptance. At the first sign of judgment or criticism they would simply disappear again. A Voice Dialogue facilitator has therefore to try to remain impartial, whatever the unconscious material that is being processed. Sometimes this is hard, for at times the voices that take the stage can be quite demonic. But the wonder is that, if they can be made to feel acceptable and loved, and if they feel that they are seen and heard, their energy then becomes transformed from negative to positive. No attempt on the part of the facilitator to "redeem" them is necessary. On the contrary, it will be a total failure. This is yet another example of the power of love to heal disharmony, and of the necessity for us to accept *whatever* is going on with us. Everything happens for a purpose. Nothing in us ever needs to be rooted out—only understood and accepted, and thereby transformed.

Affirmations for self-acceptance

I accept myself totally, just as I am.

I am not here to be perfect or to meet others' expectations.

I am good. I am enough.

The more I accept myself, the more others accept me.

Strangers are only friends to be.

I honor the needs of my Child at all times.

I am always in charge of my life.

I trust myself to be spontaneous and free.

Feeling good about myself feels totally SAFE.

I do not need to drive myself. Everything happens as it should.

I am not in this world to please others, but to please myself.

I know that I am capable of coping with every situation as it arises.

Visualizations for self-acceptance

Loving your inner child

Cast your mind back to how you were when you were little, perhaps four or five years old. See yourself as you were then, as clearly as you can.

Look deeply into the Child's eyes. See the longing there for love, unconditional and total.

Now embrace the Child. Tell it how much you love it, and that you will always be there for it, and never leave it. See how beautiful it is, how innocent and fresh.

When you have given it as much love as you know how, allow your Child to grow smaller and smaller, until it is down to a size where it will fit into your own heart.

Hold it there in your heart and, at intervals throughout the day, remind yourself that it is there, and give it lots of love.

(This beautiful and deep visualization is one of Louise Hay's. It will keep you in touch with your Inner Child and its needs.)

Your ideal self

Consider how you would really like to be. What are the qualities that you admire and envy in others that you wish you yourself had? See a person who embodies these qualities walking towards you, perhaps on a beach, or in the seclusion of your garden or on a path through the woods. As this ideal person gets closer to you he (or she) starts to slow down, and eventually stops right in front of you. You make eye contact, and you hear the other say, "I am you and you are me. You can be what I am." Feel the other's energy and the qualities that you admire so much. Then allow yourself to merge so that you become one person. Experience how it feels to be the new you, to be beautiful or strong or at peace with yourself—or whatever qualities you feel you lack and would like to have.

Stay with it for as long as feels comfortable, then allow the experience to fade.

Resolving a problem
Imagine that a problem that has been worrying you has been satisfactorily solved. See the resolution in as much detail as you can. How does it feel to no longer have that problem? Savor the relief, the joy of at last having peace of mind, and let it permeate through your body.

*Nobody heals until they get
to love themselves first.*
—Louis Nassaney, AIDS "survivor"

Chapter 5

Love Heals

Healing affirmations and visualizations

FOR ME THE MOST CONVINCING PROOF OF THE
power of loving affirmations and visualizations to
change our lives is in healing. Even deep-seated
and intractable illnesses, for example cancer, have
been found (in well-documented cases) to yield to
deliberate and persistent positive reprogramming.
If this is the case, how much more quickly and effectively can they change the way we *feel* about ourselves?

The work of Dr. Carl Simonton, radiation oncolo-
gist and medical director of the Cancer Counselling
and Research Center at Fort Worth in Texas, is well
known as the result of his bestseller, *Getting Well
Again*. He first became interested in the power of the
mind to affect the course of disease through treat-

ing female cancer patients with radiation therapy. He was struck that the women who *anticipated* the worst suffered the worst side-effects.

Simonton first used visualization therapy on a sixty-year-old man suffering from advanced throat cancer. The patient was asked to participate in a program of relaxation and visualization three times a day for five to fifteen minutes, on wakening in the morning, after lunch and at night before going to sleep. When he was sufficiently relaxed, he was asked to create mental images of his cancer cells being bombarded by the radiation therapy he was also receiving. He imagined tiny bullets of energy destroying the malignant cells, which were then removed by his body's white cells. He would end the session by visualizing the tumor shrinking in size and himself restored to radiant health. He felt better, stronger and, after two months, showed no sign of cancer.

Interestingly, this same patient used the technique to improve his arthritis, visualizing the joint surfaces becoming smooth once more. Soon he was able to go fishing again. Now thoroughly confident in his power to heal himself, he went on to cure himself of sexual impotence that had lasted over twenty years! And this is not an isolated cure. The survival rate of Simonton's patients is twice that of the US national average.

Louise Hay, the Californian who cured herself of cancer, also helps others through affirmations and visualizations. One of her "successes" has been Louis Nassaney, who healed himself of Karposi's Sarcoma under her guidance and has been in remission from AIDS ever since.

It has been found that visualizing healing is more effective if the mental pictures conjured up are friendly and non-violent. For example, visualizing sharks devouring cancer cells doesn't seem to work as well as, say, imagining a football match between the "goodies" and the "baddies" (i.e. cancer cells and helper cells), in which of course the goodies always win. Louise Hay got Nassaney to visualize the KS lesion on his thigh as a pencil mark. Every night he would create the mental image of himself erasing the lesion with a pencil rubber. He also visualized his helper cells as rabbits, reproducing themselves at a tremendous rate!

After four months the lesion began to fade and, in October 1984, a biopsy at the Los Angeles hospital where he had been treated revealed only dead scar tissue.

It is hardly surprising that orthodox medicine has begun to show interest in visualization therapy, especially where routine treatment has been proving ineffective. For example, it is now being used at one of London's great teaching hospitals, St. Mary's in Paddington.

"Dissolving patterns dissolves disease"

Louise Hay's system is based on her conviction that "dissolving patterns dissolves disease," and on the overriding importance of loving yourself. One of the exercises she recommends to counteract self-hatred is simply to look at your own reflection in a mirror daily and to say to it, "I really, really love you." She suggests that this should be done every day for at least a month and then continued "just for the joy of it." (I would add that, if you have any sort of negativity about your body, then you could do it naked, in front of a full-length mirror.)

We have to drop guilt, resentment, fear and self-loathing, and learn to love ourselves, for healing to happen, for negative feelings poison our bodies and can, sooner or later, manifest in symptoms of physical illness. Acid thoughts create acid blood.

Changing the attitudes that may have contributed to the onset of illness is also essential, otherwise our energy constellation remains the same. Even if, for example, a tumor is removed by surgery, but we still do not change the way we think and behave, it is highly likely that we will create the cancer in another part of our bodies.

We know that we create our future by what we are thinking and saying NOW, especially the thoughts about ourselves that we give credence to, and the things we say about ourselves. It is now a scientific fact that negativity depresses our immune systems and therefore lays us wide open, not only to cancer and AIDS, but to virtually any other malady as well. And, of all forms of negativity, that which we direct against ourselves is the most lethal. If we are attacked from outside at least (hopefully) we can defend ourselves. But if the enemy is within, in the form of self-hatred and self-recrimination, there can be no one there to defend us. And, predictably (since our bodies mirror our psychic realities), our *internal* defense system (i.e. our immune system) gets just as depressed as our minds.

Love and immunity

Bernie Siegel MD, Assistant Clinical Professor of Surgery at Yale Medical School, says categorically, in his book, *Love, Medicine and Miracles*,

> The simple truth is, happy people generally don't get sick ... I am convinced that unconditional love is the most powerful known stimulant of the immune system. If I told patients to raise their blood levels of immune globulins or killer T-cells, no one would know how. But if I can teach them to love themselves and others fully, the same changes happen automatically. The truth is, love heals.

Even watching romantic films helps to boost the immune system, as Harvard psychologists David McClelland and Carol Kirshnit established in 1982. Watching such movies was found to increase levels of immunoglobulin-A in the saliva, our first line of defense against colds and other viral diseases. The same researchers found that a documentary on the work of Mother Teresa of Calcutta produced an immediate and appreciable rise of immunoglobulin levels in the saliva of viewers, quite unrelated to their conscious like or dislike of her. Dr McClelland also tells us that even just thinking of loving experiences of the past, of loving and feeling loved, increases immunoglobulin levels.

Our immune systems are thus profoundly affected by both the energy, positive or negative, that we ourselves put out, and by that which comes at us from the outside. A combination of self-love, affirmations and visualizations (as well as, of course, nourishing our bodies with good food, exercise and fresh air) would seem to be an essential daily discipline for anybody who is ill or vulnerable.

I have a counselling client who is HIV-positive. He was alarmed when his doctor told him that at his last blood test his helper cell count was shown to have gone down to the very low level of 184, and he was told that it would be advisable for him to start taking Retrovir. For the next month he used visualization, cut out stress and generally treated himself more gently than he had hitherto.

He visualized his little helper cells flowing along on a stream (his blood). Sitting on the banks of the stream were frogs who gobbled up the viruses embedded in the cells. A flock of Disney-type little birds would then descend on the cells and divide them up with their beaks so that they multiplied. My client had set himself a goal of doubling up his count by the next test of his immune status. To his surprise and delight the next test revealed that he had more than achieved his goal. The total number of his helper cells had increased to no less than 684! His doctor was also surprised when I spoke to him later about the case. An AIDS specialist himself, he confessed that in all his experience he had never seen such a remarkable improvement in a patient.

Loving and forgiving

We can affirm and visualize until we are blue in the face, but unless we love ourselves it is unlikely that

we will get very far, for our negative attitudes will
drain away the positive energy we have been building up. It really does seem that St. Paul was right:
Faith and Hope are important, but the greatest of
all is Love.

A big part of love is forgiveness. In fact, it is
impossible for us to love unless we *do* forgive—over
and over again. The connection between the development of cancer and the holding on to resentments
has long been established. Dr. Carl Simonton and his
wife Stephanie found in a survey that the typical
cancer patient evinces a strong tendency to hold on
to resentment and a reluctance to forgive. Earlier,
New York psychologist Lawrence LeShan, in a survey of 250 cancer patients, came up with a "cancer
profile." He found that they all suffered from feelings of self-hatred and an inability to come to their
own defense if attacked. They also suffered tension
in their relationships with their parents.

Healing is the outward sign of the restoration
to inner harmony and balance. Hatred, whether of
others or of ourselves, destroys our peace of mind,
which should actually be our top priority. Forgiveness does not mean that we condone injustice: it
simply means letting go of negative attitudes that
can make us ill and unhappy. In Chapter 9 I shall
be suggesting how this can be done, together with
letting go of the past, in spite of the part of us
that still wants to hang on to grudges and a sense
of grievance. It is worth doing. In fifty-seven well-
documented "cancer miracles" quoted by Professor
Siegel, the cures followed the conscious decision of

the patients to give up their anger and depression. From that point their tumors started to shrink.

Affirmations for healing

I KNOW that I have the power to heal my body and create perfect, radiant health.

I am divinely protected from all infection.

Every day, in every way, I am getting better and better.

I feel well, I look well, I AM well.

I am willing to drop any mental pattern that's making me ill.

I no longer need to be ill.

With every breath I feel more alive.

There is no limit to how good I can feel.

I love and approve of myself every moment.

I love and approve of my body.

My body is full of light and totally clear.

I feel strong and brimming with energy.

My immune system grows stronger every day.

I deserve to enjoy radiant health.

Every hand that touches my body is a healing hand.

My doctors are amazed at my rapid recovery.

My treatment is healing me: there are no side-effects.

My [name the part of your body that is suffering] *is healing rapidly.*

I forgive everybody whom I mistakenly thought tried to hurt me.

Visualizations for healing

1. Create a picture in your mind of the part of your body that needs to be healed. See, in any way that feels right, that healing happening. Finish by seeing the sick part totally healthy again.

2. See yourself restored to perfect health. How does it feel to be strong again, to have plenty of energy and a good appetite? Dwell on this picture and recall it (and the feeling that goes with it) during the day.

3. Whenever you go to the lavatory, imagine that all the body's toxins, impurities and germs are being flushed out of your body. (I have found that the image of a swimming pool being hosed down and all the dirt disappearing down the drain is a good one.)

4. Imagine a bright, clear, white light streaming down from above. It enters your body through your head and out again through your toes. Feel this light cleansing, purifying and strengthening every part of your body.

5. Call to mind, one after another, all the people you know who love you, and wish that you could get healed. Hear them telling you they love you and wish you well again. Allow their loving energy to reach you. FEEL it. Finish by gathering all these friends and lovers together. Thank them, and express your own love for them too. (This is a visualization recommended by the internationally-known healer Martin Brofman, a former Wall Street executive who healed himself of throat cancer in 1975.)

Be to yourself
As you would to your friend
—*King Henry VIII, I.i*, Shakespeare

Chapter 6

Nourishing Yourself

Physical nourishment

IF WE LOVE OURSELVES UNCONDITIONALLY, we will nourish ourselves. We will want to treat our bodies with respect, supplying it with the food it needs to stay healthy, giving it exercise and fresh air, avoiding excesses and addictions to things that bring it down. Most of us now know something about what a healthy diet is, the importance of a basically vegetarian, whole-grain diet, and the avoidance of red meat and foods high in cholesterol, sugar and additives. Never before have so many people been aware of the connection between what we put into our mouths and our state of health.

And beyond this, there is also a growing awareness of eating disorders. People are examining their eating habits and the way they relate to food, and becoming aware of the issues underlying nourishment and food abuse.

If we have a low self-image and are unable to love ourselves unconditionally, we may abuse and try to control ourselves through food. Anorexics obsessively deny themselves nourishment. Bulimics suppress negative feelings by over-eating and then guiltily throwing it all back up again. Overeaters try to fill the gaps in their lives by eating, but they can't get enough.

What we need to do is learn how to shift our perspectives on food. We need to look at our nutrient and calorie intake, but we also need to see how our eating patterns reflect our attitudes to our emotional and spiritual nourishment as well.

Taking a good look at your diet and recognizing, as the yogis say, that "we are what we eat," is an important step for anyone who wants to be their own best friend.

It is impossible to generalize about the "right" diet because everyone is different, but here are some points to watch out for when thinking about improving your eating habits.

- Are you missing or skimping meals?
- Do you eat too much?
- Are you getting enough protein?
- Are you getting enough vitamins (especially vitamin B) and minerals?
- Do you eat too much sugar?
- Are you getting enough fiber?
- Do you drink enough water (2 to 3 liters) during the day?

- Do you drink too much alcohol?
- Are you allowing yourself time to digest your food properly?

Spiritual nourishment

We also need other forms of nourishment apart from what our bodies demand. Mother Teresa has talked about "spiritual deprivation," where our spirits do not receive enough nourishment. Our minds, emotions—in short our *spirits*—need also be nurtured if we are to experience true well-being. We are all "bodyminds" and neglect of the more subtle areas of our being will sooner or later lead to the development of physical symptoms in our bodies. As we saw in Chapter 5, this is the way illness is generated, from the inside out. A malaise in our aura (the subtle energy field that surrounds all of us for about an arm's-length from our bodies), if unchecked, can develop into full-blown illness. If we are sufficiently in tune with ourselves, our inner wisdom will tell us that something is not quite right. Ill-health is always preceded by feelings of being "down," of something being wrong, of depression and fatigue. Disease is always far advanced before ever it manifests on the physical plane.

Feel well and be well

In 1957 Sir Heneage Ogilvie, the consulting surgeon at Guy's Hospital in London, startled his colleagues by asserting that "the happy man [or woman] never gets cancer." His remark echoes that of Sir James Paget, who in the last century stated that his view that the real cause of cancer was disappointment.

Enjoying ourselves would seem to be prophylactic. The best way to *be* well is to *feel* well. Humor, not taking things too seriously, is very much a part of getting and staying well. This was the experience of Norman Cousins, author of the best-selling book, *Anatomy of an Illness*. Cousins suffered from a painful, incurable disease called ankylosing spondylitis (a disease of the body's connective tissues), and had been given up as a hopeless case by his doctors. But he started to get better when he moved out of hospital and spent the day in his hotel room laughing at videos of *Candid Camera* and old Marx brothers films. For him laughter did indeed prove to be "the best medicine," helped by high doses of vitamin C.

Loving people

Experiencing loving and being loved can also bring about miracles of healing. As we have seen, even meditating on these experiences using visualizations improves our immune system. One of the main ways, therefore, of loving ourselves is to surround ourselves as much as we can with loving, caring, sensitive people, people with "good vibrations." And the more we allow ourselves to live by love, the more love comes our way. We get the energy we put out back, multiplied.

Always make sure you are offloading positive energy on to others, not negative. Try to interact with your friends by "laddering." This means taking it in turns to put out positive and loving messages to each other. And give people the freedom of the following:

- your full attention when they are speaking;
- make eye contact;
- share their spaces—even if you don't agree with or understand them;
- don't contradict or judge them.

Remember to share *feelings* and try always to find something positive to say, for negativity contracts and dampens any loving vibration.

It is always better to avoid people who are negative, constantly complaining about how awful everybody else is, how badly they are treated and so forth. They are creating their own misery by their addiction to victim consciousness. Don't let them bring you down too. Learn how to say "No" to them.

Being and feeling

Really, nourishing yourself is about wanting to give yourself nourishing, satisfying experiences, and also to avoid giving yourself a hard time in any way. As well as ensuring that the energy you put out into the world is clear and positive, it is also about *balance*. One of the ways most of us are unbalanced is in our compulsive *doing*. We rarely allow ourselves just to *be*.

We need to learn how to relax, properly, in order to get back in touch with ourselves and give ourselves real nourishment for our senses. When we really relax we are able to let go of what W. B. Cannon, the neurologist, called the "fight or flight" response and sink into what Dr. Herbert Benson, a researcher into the mechanics of tension and relaxation, called the "relaxation response."

When this happens changes occur in brainwave activity that are quite different from sleep patterns. This can be measured using an electroencephalograph (EEG), which reveals that most of our waking state we are operating on the beta wavelength, meaning that electrical activity in the brain registers within the range 14 to 26Hz (cycles per second). And if we are stressed this level rises on the beta scale, and we begin to feel uptight or "speedy." The famous "fight or flight" response is high beta.

During relaxation the brainwaves start to slow down to a lower range of frequencies (from 8 to 13Hz) and we reach a state that is called "alpha." It can be described as "that holiday feeling" or a feeling of having space around us and no pressure. The more relaxed we become, the deeper we go into alpha, and the more we feel the benefits of this blissful state, and can recharge our batteries.

When we are in beta, on the other hand, it is true that we get things done. But beta is not blissful, whereas alpha is. The royal road out of beta into alpha is through *feeling*. We need to get back in touch with our bodies, and to give ourselves time and space to tune into our own processes. This can often be blotted out by the manifold pressures from the outside world, that Taoist sages called the "Ten Thousand Things." We are constantly assailed by them, with the result that we lose touch with who we are and what we are feeling. As Fritz Perls, founder of Gestalt Therapy (see Chapter 4) put it, we need to "lose our minds and come back to our senses."

Take some time every day to treat yourself to a session of deep relaxation, perhaps using the Deep Relaxation method outlined in Chapter 8.

There are many other ways in which you can nourish yourself through relaxation, and everybody will have their own ideas about what relaxes them best when they are feeling tense. Some people enjoy gardening, or otherwise communing with nature. Walking in the countryside, or swimming in the sea makes many of us feel fresh again, and cleansed at some very deep level. And contemplating the beauty and perfection of nature, for example a spectacular sunset, are aesthetic experiences to be valued. For some, indeed, they afford what can only be called religious experiences, in that they remind us that we are all part of the Whole.

In this connection it may be mentioned that prayer is also deeply nourishing. It reminds us of our "at-one-ment" with the Universe, and recharges our spiritual batteries. It has been said that "Prayer does not change God; it changes *us*," and when we are plagued by constant anxiety, grieving over loss, desperately ill or crushed by misfortune, it is virtually the only thing that can help. To surrender to the "will of God" when all else is collapsing about us is, paradoxically, empowering. Even the physical structure that goes with some forms of prayer can enhance the relaxing, nourishing effect: sitting or kneeling in a quiet place, candlelight, soft organ music, eyes closed, repeating invocations etc.

Enjoy!

Music
Music, too, "the food of love," is akin to prayer in that it stimulates our heart center, and has a purifying effect on us. It is also one of the easiest ways for many people to get into the alpha state, as well as lowering blood pressure, slowing the pulse rate and increasing the flow of gastric juices. Although taste in music is a personal thing, studies have shown that the particular rhythms of baroque music and especially Mozart are the most relaxing, because they reflect the frequencies found in the alpha state. You may also like to try New Age instrumental music.

Exercise
Since most of us spend so much of our working day "in our heads," i.e. having to think, plan, calculate and relate on a business level, any activity in off-duty hours that serves to bring us back "into our bodies" is bound to come as something of a relief and help to restore the balance. This, of course, accounts for much of the present popularity of running, jogging and aerobics. Dancing is an ideal form of exercise. To dance is to celebrate *having* a body and being alive in this world. Flowing with the music centers us. Expressing ourselves freely revives stagnant energy. Above all, it is enjoyable, and, as we have said, to do anything you really *enjoy* doing is deeply nourishing.

"Come to your senses"

By using a bit of imagination, we can make enjoyable, nourishing experiences out of the most mundane, ordinary things. Bathing, for example, can be transformed from a daily mechanical ritual into a deliciously sensual experience, and thus help us to "come to our senses," as well as providing us with deep relaxation and space. A lighted candle beside the bathtub, fragrant oil in the water, soothing background music, can all help to make us feel good, which is what self-nourishment is all about.

A relaxing massage afterwards can help you relax and be a pleasurable and sensual experience. If you live a hectic lifestyle, ask a friend to give you a massage on a regular basis.

Environment

One of the most obvious ways in which we can show our love for ourselves is the sort of environment with which we surround ourselves. We have already looked at the importance of being with people who have good vibrations if we possibly can. Our living environment is equally important. To create a home in which you feel safe, that is comfortable, bright and welcoming is one of the best things you can do for yourself. Our surroundings reflect us, and we in turn are affected by them.

An effective way to improve your frame of mind if you are feeling depressed is to put energy into cleaning up your living space. The more untidy (or worse, dirty) it is, the worse you will feel. Not only will your mood lighten up after a session of cleaning, polishing and restoring order, but so will the place itself. And the more energy you put into it, the more it will *shine*. Make it a place you are happy to invite your friends into, to fill it with love and good vibrations. Make it a space *they* will enjoy coming into, with plants and flowers, soft lighting, comfortable seating and nice music.

And once you have finished cleaning up your living space, pay some attention to your external appearance. Love yourself by pampering yourself a little: a new haircut, outfit, even a manicure can work wonders for your self-esteem. And remember, do it to please yourself first.

Affirmations for nourishment

Things always work out, so they must be working out NOW.

"All is well, and all manner of thing shall be well." (Revelation from the medieval English mystic Julian of Norwich in 1373)

Thy will, not mine be done.

I surrender to the will of God.

Being good to myself feels totally SAFE.

I nourish myself at least as well as I nourish others.

Because I love myself,
  I nourish my body with good food, sleep and exercise.
  I provide myself only with good experiences.
  I create a graceful living space for myself.
  I allow myself to relax whenever I need to.
  I do only what I enjoy doing.
  I choose to be only with positive, nourishing people.

Visualization for nourishment

Call to mind the times in your life when you have felt deeply contented, when all was right with the world. Try and recapture how it felt. See it in as much detail as possible. Where were you? What were you doing? Who were you with (if anybody)? Why was the experience so satisfying for you?

Chapter 7

Be Here Now

"Knowing" and "thinking about"

WE CAN SET UP ANY NUMBER OF PLEASANT experiences for ourselves in the interests of self-nourishment, but unless we are really *present* our efforts will go to nought. There will not be anyone there to enjoy them. Your body may be present, but you will be somewhere else. That somewhere else is most likely to be in your head, lost in thinking, worrying about something perhaps, or simply already moving on in your imagination to the *next* experience. We are where our attention is. The expression "being here now" is the central tenet of Zazen meditation which concentrates on staying present-centered. For more on Zazen and meditation in general, see Chapter 8.

We rarely allow ourselves to experience totally

where we are. We move from experience A to experience B, like butterflies, constantly flittering from one thing to another, never truly savoring the satisfaction that *this* moment is bringing. To allow ourselves to experience this satisfaction we have to learn to allow ourselves to move from A1 to A2 to A3, rather than from A straight to B, in other words to *feel* each experience in more depth, to savor it more fully, through our senses rather than through the filter of the mind. "Knowing" is not the same as "thinking about."

The development of language, of reading, was a gigantic step in the evolution and development of consciousness of the human race. It made communication simpler, faster, clearer. We have learned to use symbols for things, and this bypasses the need, each time we want to refer to something, to have to describe it to another. Words are a form of shorthand, and everybody knows what they stand for. But the menu is not the meal. And eating the menu will not satisfy our hunger.

There is a saying in Zen which goes, "Let the mind have no abiding place." It is only when we can let go of our fixed ideas about the way things *should* be, that we become open enough to experience things *as they are*. When we look at a rose, for example, we will not savor its uniqueness if we are thinking *about* it, what species it is, how perfect it is, what blemishes there are and so forth. These judgments act like a filter that stops us from experiencing *this* rose directly, for its fragrance, its texture, its color. And so we miss the total, fresh experience of "roseness." This is how most of us live most of our lives, only half-experiencing everything, simply because we are not open to the new. We are always making comparisons with how it used to be in the past, judging, labelling, pigeonholing. This is how we continually miss *intensity* of experience. And then we wonder why life seems repetitive and drab.

This is as true of relationships as for roses. We take our partners for granted, we think we know them, and relate to them out of habit and the past, instead of allowing them to surprise us. And then we wonder where the romance went, why we are bored, why everything seems so stale and predictable. It is because we are so stuck in the past that we do not allow ourselves to be reborn to each other every day, every moment. For nothing in life is ever fixed: it is a constant becoming. And always new.

Letting go of the past

We have already touched on the importance of letting go of the past, and learning to forgive, if we want to stay well. Not only does hanging on to it make us stale, it makes us old, and it can even make us ill. Hanging on to past resentments and bitterness has been shown to be particularly lethal. Acid thoughts create acid blood that can eat away at our vitals. Research by Dr. Carl Simonton and others indicates that there is a strong correlation between unwillingness to forgive and the onset of cancer, for example. It has been also suggested by Caroline Myss, medical clairvoyant and journalist, that it is no accident that the high-risk groups for AIDS are people who feel themselves to be social outcasts, who have developed a victim-consciousness and who feel unsafe in this world: male homosexuals, heroin addicts, prostitutes, and the inhabitants of Africa, the most victimized part of our planet. Continually feeling oneself to be an outsider, not belonging, or being rejected or unacceptable, depresses our immune system like nothing else can. Yet in truth there are no "outsiders;" we all belong. This is our home.

Much of the reason why we are continually sucked back into dwelling on the past, rather than staying in the present, is due to what in Gestalt Therapy (see Chapter 4) is called our "unfinished business." This simply means that situations in the past, which were not resolved at the time, hover around like ghosts to haunt us in the present. Experiences that have been completed, that we have worked through, vanish without trace. What we experience totally, disappears from our consciousness and will not trouble us any more. We won't even remember it.

It is important to be constantly clearing unfinished business, to exorcise the demons of guilt, resentment and fear, so that we can stay available to the new. Forgiving past hurts—and forgiving yourself, over and over again—confronting your fear, reappraising the ideas about yourself that you took on board when you were too young to know how toxic they were, is a constant "spring cleaning" of your psyche that will free you from the past.

Other people can be a big help in allowing you to do this, provided they can *listen* without judging to what you have to say. This is what therapy and counselling is about. Often a good friend whom you trust will be a great help, and certainly a lot cheaper than a therapist!

But there are also techniques you can use by yourself to bring about transformation of the way you see things, including the affirmations and visualizations at the end of this chapter.

The "mind's abiding place" can equally well be our expectations of what is to come, rather than our memories of what is past. We can sacrifice living in the moment by continually living in the future. When we do so we are preferring the world of fantasy to the world of reality. And often our fantasies are anxiety- and doom-laden. There is a vast difference between using fantasy creatively, as when we visualize, and scaring ourselves with catastrophic expectations.

Fear of the future

Behind all avoidance of living in the present is *fear*. However painful our memories are, at least they are familiar. We know where we are with them and what to expect. The thing we all fear most is the unknown. And living in the present means to tolerate not-knowing, and to live without structures. Flight into the future is a denial of the emptiness we would otherwise be stuck with. In this emptiness all manner of scary feelings have a chance to surface, to impinge on our consciousness. To avoid this we try to escape, and in so doing run away from our selves.

It is true that we never know what the future

holds for us. So what alternative do we have to panicking about it? The answer is to learn to *trust* that whatever happens is good, and that the Universe is not out to "get" us. It is benevolent, and on our side. It is also true that it gives us the power to create our future from moment to moment. It leaves us free to create either nightmares or bliss with our thoughts. It is up to us. Once you have done something that was setting up a wall of fear within you, you will feel wonderful—and wonder why you experienced such powerful and negative feelings.

Abiding in the Now, taking things as they come, experiencing them fully, being willing to accept yourself and your situation and working through any difficulties, rather than taking flight into fantasies of the past or the future, is what living fully is all about. It has been called "the sacrament of the moment."

Some people find that "body work" can put them back in touch with the Now. If you get a chance to experience shiatsu, massage or Applied Kinesiology, for example, you will find it a wonderfully "grounding" experience.

Affirmations for being here now

I trust that whatever happens is good.

God wants me to be happy.

My future is bright, safe, healthy, prosperous and loving.

I have dropped the past and am free.

I let go of all limiting or negative ideas that create negative effects in my life.

I let go of all resentment, grief and guilt.

I forgive everybody I mistakenly thought tried to hurt me.

I am grateful for the miracles that happen every day.

Life gets better and better every day.

I am divinely protected.

I am not my mother. I do not have her thoughts and feelings.

I am not my father. I do not have his thoughts and feelings.

I am not my teachers, or their ideas.

I forgive my parents, from the bottom of my heart.

Everything is perfection when I stay in the Now.

Visualizations for being here now

"Grounding" visualization
Sit in a chair with your back straight but relaxed,

and your feet uncrossed, soles flat on the floor. Close your eyes, take a few deep breaths, and focus on the very base of your spinal cord. Visualize your spinal cord slowly lengthening downwards, dividing into two branches or roots that pass slowly down both legs. Feel your feet planted firmly on the floor as the roots pass through them and down into the earth. Deeper and deeper they go, making you feel "rooted," "grounded," solid and securely based . . . Enjoy this safe feeling for a while as you watch the main roots putting out secondary roots, spreading out under the earth . . . Now feel the energy from the Earth spreading up slowly through those roots into the soles of your feet. Imagine that this energy is molten red, like lava from a volcano. Feel it warming you as it passes up your legs and the two "branches" join up again at the base of your spine.

Stay with this feeling of being "rooted" in the ground and nourished by Mother Earth, and enjoy how "solid" and safe you feel.

Letting go of fear
See fear as a black cloud that hovers above your head, and to which you are attached by a string. Now let go of the string and watch the black cloud of fear as it floats away, getting smaller the higher it goes. Keep watching it until it is so far away that you can no longer see it.

Unfinished business
This visualization is useful for working through a painful experience from the past. Remember that whatever you allow yourself to experience *totally*,

will disappear. It is used in Applied Kinesiology, one of the manipulative therapies, used to transmit or arouse healing energy in the body.

Sit at a table with the fingers of both hands on your forehead. Keep your eyes closed. Recall to mind the distressing event of the past that you would like to work through. See it in as much detail as possible, where you were, who said what, what happened *exactly*. Above all, how it felt. Go over it again and again, allowing yourself to feel the pain, the fear, or whatever comes up for you. Remember and trust that these are only memories and cannot hurt you. Face them and they will lose their power over you.

You will know when to stop, for you will feel "finished." Sit quietly for a while, and allow any reappraisal to come up. You may have to repeat the process later on to extract any "juice" or unfinished business that remains.

Chapter 8

Give Yourself Space!

Psychic space

IT HAS LONG SEEMED TO ME THAT THE amount of space one has in this world is directly related to one's position in the social pecking order. The richer you are, the bigger the house you can afford; the more famous you are, the more elaborate the precautions against intrusions on your privacy. We are not even supposed to *speak* to royalty unless they address us first, presumably to safeguard the "divinity that doth hedge a king" (or a queen). At the other end of the scale, of course, poverty and overcrowded living conditions go together.

But space is not just about how many rooms you have in your house. Over and above purely physical space there is also *psychic* space. I would hazard a guess that the latter is something most of us don't

feel we have enough of. Working for a living, shopping, cooking, worrying, we are all constantly under
pressure to "keep it all together." Things that we
are supposed to be doing in the interests of survival present themselves one after another. When
one task is completed another leaps up to take its
place. There is just no let up with demands on our
time and energy (especially if we have children),
except for the blessed two or three weeks in the year
when we take a well-earned holiday to "get away
from it all"—with the children in tow. Sometimes,
in fact, the only way we can get some respite from
too much stress and pressure is to go down with flu
or a streaming cold and take to our beds. Illness
is virtually the only reason for downing tools that
is generally recognized as valid by employers and
families!

Much of what we are required to do is unavoid-
able, and if we want to keep our jobs or care for
our loved ones, we do it, with more or less grace.
What can be changed, however, is *how* we do what
we have to do, and if we are alert to the necessity
of recharging our batteries from time to time before
we get back to the grindstone *we can do it*. We
must recognize that we live in a world where sheer
pace is the order of the day, and those of us who
live in cities are constantly bombarded by noise (a
form of pollution), demands on our attention from
traffic, advertisements and other forms of sensory
over-stimulation. We need to take "breathing space,"
and to "give ourselves a break" from all this. If we
don't, we run the risk of falling prey to any of the
"stress diseases" to which we may be vulnerable.

Don't overdo it

Loving yourself, taking back your power, not being a victim, is very much about becoming aware of your own energy levels and choosing not to over-extend yourself. This has to be done *before* you start getting drained by listening to the inner voice that tells you when you are "overdoing it." Ignore that inner voice and you are in trouble. Give yourself time to check out internally whether you really want to accept any more commitments, especially if other people's time limits are involved. Don't over-extend yourself: set your *own* boundaries. Learn when to say "No."

There are several ways in which we can "blow" our energy and end up feeling drained. One is by resistance to the job in hand. Either do it with gusto, or don't do it at all. This applies equally to social as to work situations. If half of you doesn't want to be where you are, doing what you are doing, the other half of you just doesn't have the energy to get on with it, for it is being drained away. This we experience subjectively as fatigue. We never get tired when we are enjoying ourselves, simply because our energy flows freely into the activity that interests us.

Have you ever found yourself at a social gathering, feeling you would rather not be there, and wondering how you managed to get yourself roped into going in the first place. If this sounds familiar, you will remember how endless the occasion seems, how irritating or boring the small-talk going on around you can be, how you have to rack your brains to find something to say to people. This is the experience that *you* have given *yourself* because you were not clear with yourself about what you wanted, whether to enjoy other people's company or just be on your own. Either choice can be good, so long as you do it *totally*. In other words, if you have chosen to be with people, really *be* with them. Otherwise you won't enjoy it, and neither will they. Don't wobble.

How often do we refuse ourselves permission to decline invitations, either because we think people will be offended or disappointed, or because we don't want to be thought unsociable. And, sometimes, we can be afraid of solitude and silence, and confuse being alone with being lonely. However, these are two different things altogether: aloneness is enjoying your own presence, whereas loneliness is missing others.

Enjoying your alone-ness

If we can learn to enjoy our own alone-ness good things can happen. Our batteries recharge themselves, for we are not leaking out energy in unnecessary chit-chat. In times of silence we get more in touch with our own inner process and intuition, which is usually, during a hectic working day, blotted out by all the demands on our attention (which is our energy being pulled out by external stimuli). Yet silence, like space, is something of a luxury today. We are unused to having it. Some of us, indeed, are afraid of it.

The more we are exposed to the hurly-burly of the world outside, the more we feel the need for a bit of silence, to be left to re-establish communication with ourselves for a while. For example, when we arrive home from work, the nicest thing those we live with can do for us is just to leave us alone for a while. Unfortunately, our loved ones are often unaware of just how frazzled we feel. With the best of intentions they offer to make tea, and bombard us with questions about our working day. At least it *sounds* like bombardment to us.

For example, I have a friend who supports her old, widowed mother and goes out to work. Though she loves her mother and cares for her very well, she is driven to distraction by being fussed over as soon as she walks in the front door after a day's work followed by shopping on the way home. The mother, of course, has been by herself all day and needs a bit of contact, exactly what her daughter has had too much of. They are therefore both in totally different and opposite spaces. What is the solution? To ask for space from her mother, a woman of another genera-tion who never had any herself while bringing up her family, would not probably be understood and would smack of rejection of what was well intended. Too often this results in feelings of injury on the part of the mother (who retires to her room and sulks) and guilt on the part of her daughter.

One answer might be to say "I want to take a bath or a shower"—and withdraw. The privacy of the bathroom, at least, is still respected in our culture. To say that "I was in the bathroom" is the per-fect excuse for not answering the phone, or the door-bell. There is simply no comeback. It is virtually the only place left where one can count on being alone for a while without upsetting anyone.

You have to be quite tough sometimes to get space for yourself. Others do not usually *give* us space. Often they don't even understand the concept. We have to *take* it for ourselves when we feel we need to, sometimes at the risk of disappointing others' expectations. After all, do you want to please them, or do you want to please yourself? If you don't give yourself enough space, then stress can easily build.

One way to love yourself and enjoy your aloneness is to structure a period every day when you can withdraw and relax totally, at least for half an hour or so. It will make all the difference in the world to how you feel, physically and psychologically. As well as antidoting the stress that has been building up during your working day, it will sweeten your humour and make you easier to live with. There is a close correlation between lack of space and aggression. The less space, the more aggression.

You can spend this time which you have claimed for yourself either in practising deep relaxation, or in meditation.

1. Deep relaxation

Basically, deep relaxation (or the alpha technique, see Chapter 6) is about progressively letting go of tension in the muscles and allowing your awareness to come out of your head and back into your body by giving your attention to bodily sensations.

Make sure that you will not be disturbed for at least half an hour; also that the room is warm enough. Loosen your clothing and take off your shoes. Turn down the lighting so that the room is dimly lit. Some people like to wear a blindfold. Lie on your back either on a firm mattress or on a carpeted floor with your head either unsupported or resting on a low pillow. Your arms should be at your sides, palms up or down—whichever feels more relaxed.

Start the relaxation process by picturing in your mind a place where you can be alone, comfortable and perfectly safe (see the garden and beach visualizations at the end of this chapter).

Take a few deep, slow breaths, and start repeating silently the word "Relax" as you exhale. Have the intention to set aside for a while any problems with which you may have been preoccupied and tell yourself you will deal with them later.

Listen to the sounds from the outside world that come to you as you lie there with your eyes closed, without trying to identify them or wishing they were not there. Feel your body getting heavier and heavier and allow the mattress or the floor to take over the responsibility for supporting your weight.

As you sink into the floor let your mouth drop open and the muscles of your face sag. Give yourself permission to really *feel* how tired you are, and let this show in your expression. Become aware of your breathing, and breathe through your mouth from now on.

Start now to encourage energy to come down out of your head and thinking, by giving attention to the body and *feeling*. Focus in turn on the various parts of the body. Take your time. Begin with the toes of the left foot. Don't "wiggle" them, just feel them "from the inside," one toe after the other.

Now feel the rest of the left foot in turn: your heel pressing into the floor or mattress; the sensitive sole; the hard bones above the instep. Now feel the weight of the whole foot. Imagine it getting heavier and sinking into the floor.

Next, move on to the left ankle. Feel its shape and the hard protuberances on each side of it, then move on upwards. Feel the shinbone, its length and hardness. Tense up the muscle of the calf and then relax it. Tense it up again and relax it again.

Let your attention move up the rest of your left leg: kneecap; thigh . . . Tighten the thigh muscle and relax it again. Now feel the whole of your left leg getting heavier and heavier, sinking down. Feel the difference between the left leg that you have just untensed and the right, unrelaxed leg.

After a few moments, go through the relaxing process again, this time with the right leg, starting with the toes. Enjoy the blissful sensation of heaviness in your limbs which will start spreading throughout the rest of your body even before you begin working to relax the other parts. The technique is the same all over: if it is a muscle, first tighten it then relax it, tighten it again and relax it again—and allow it to get heavier. Otherwise, feel the part as much as you can, its shape, its size, its texture. The constant theme, whatever part is involved, is "heaviness, letting-go, sinking down" . . .

When the legs are totally relaxed, continue with the following sequence:

pelvis
genitals
lower back

spine
chest
shoulders
left arm (upper, elbow, forearm, wrist)
left hand (palm, thumb, fingers)
right arm (upper, elbow, forearm, wrist)
right hand (palm, thumb, fingers)

Move on to the belly, allowing it to soften and "melt." Allow plenty of time for this, for we hold a lot of tension in this area.

Lastly, work on relaxing the muscles of the face. Let go of tension around the eyes, jaw, mouth, tongue.

By now you will be blissfully relaxed at a deep level. Enjoy it for as long as you can. Stay untensed by continuing to focus your attention on your body sensations. Accept whatever is happening, allow it to just be there. LET GO.

An "alpha a day" does indeed help keep the doctor away.

2. Meditation

Meditation is similar to deep relaxation. But whereas deep relaxation is aimed primarily at relaxing the body by untensing tight muscles, meditation seeks to restore peace of mind by stopping the chaotic flow of thoughts and ideas, and the internal chatter that goes on in our heads all the time. Of course, since mind and body are not two separate things, but parts of the same energy continuum, there will be an overlap. Relaxing the body will quieten the mind; quietening the mind will serve to relax tension in the body.

Whether you decide to use your "giving yourself space" session for deep relaxation or to meditating is up to you. There are many meditation techniques and you can experiment with them to find out which technique suits you best. Here are a few time-honored ones. Others you can find in my *Meditation for Everybody*, listed in the recommended Further Reading list at the end of this book.

Meditation Technique 1: Zazen
Zazen means "just sitting," and staying present-centered (the main theme of this chapter).

Sit in a comfortable position, either on a chair, or on a cushion, and be sure to keep your back straight without straining. Just as in deep relaxation where you gave your attention to what was happening in your body, so in Zazen you simply allow outside sounds and other stimuli to reach you without doing anything about them, considering them or evaluating them. Just let them be there. If they become loud or intrusive, don't get angry or wish they would stop. Include them as part of what is going on. Zazen is the central discipline of Zen Buddhism and consists in merely practising "being here now."

Meditation Technique 2: Vipassana
Vipassana means "watching the breath." Don't change your normal breathing pattern—just become aware of it. Focus your attention on the tip of your nose, feeling the incoming and outgoing breath through your nostrils. Giving attention to your

breathing will automatically slow down the train
of your thoughts, and relieve you from preoccupa-
tion with the thoughts and images cluttering up
your mind. By and by, you will start to enjoy the
stillness and relief that comes from letting go of your
worries and busy-ness and allowing yourself just to
be for a change. For this is all that meditation is,
just being in the Now. It is like coming home to
yourself again. The more often you meditate, the
easier it gets to slip into the alpha state and out
of beta.

Meditation Technique 3: Tratak
Tratak is a Hindu word which means "gazing." It
is a device (like all meditation techniques) for
slowing down the thought process by encouraging
one-pointedness. It is easier to get off a carousel
when it starts to slow down rather than trying to
leap off it while it is revolving at full speed.

Sit quietly and comfortably and just let your eyes
rest on some predetermined object of contemplation.
It doesn't much matter what this is, so long as it is
not disturbing in any way. Traditionally, the flame
of a lighted candle is used, but it could be flowers,
a devotional image, a photograph of a loved one, or
whatever you like.

Don't strain your eyes: it is quite unnecessary.
Keep them soft and unfocused. You are not trying to
see anything special, but just looking, as if you were
sitting on the top deck of a bus going down Oxford
Street and idly observing the crowds without much
interest in who is doing what.

Staying meditative

By and by, once you get the hang of it (and meditation is really only a knack), you will begin to experience longer and longer periods of relief from the incessant internal chatter in your head, and more and more inner stillness and peace. The following tips will help you to stay centered and in touch with yourself in the course of your working day:

- Stay in the present. Stop your mind from wandering into the past or the future.
- Be one-pointed. Do one thing at a time and give it your total attention.
- Don't think unless you have to. Rather, FEEL the world around you.
- Don't leak energy unnecessarily. Talk only when you want to.

Affirmations for space

I give myself permission to take my space whenever I need to.

I no longer need to rush.

I have all the time in the world.

I enjoy what I do—otherwise I don't do it.

I am the center of my world.

I have as much right to be here as anybody else.

I do not accept anyone else's "shoulds" but my own.

It's OK for me to relax and take it easy. I deserve it.

I am not in this world to meet others' expectations.

It really is OK for me to say "No."

Stress is a thing of the past.

Visualization for space

(*Note*: This visualization can be used during your relaxation period, or at the start of your meditation session to quieten your mind. It is also useful when everything around you is very hectic (for example at work) if you can snatch a few minutes by yourself. If necessary, go and hide away in the toilet!)

Conjure up a picture of a place that is peaceful. It can be an actual place that you remember, or an imaginary setting. The main thing is that you feel SAFE there and will be undisturbed. Here are a couple of examples.

1. Beach
Create a clear picture in your mind of a secluded beach. See yourself lazing in the sunshine and feel the warmth of the sun's rays on your body. The only sounds that you can hear are the sounds of nature, for there is nobody else on your beach. Listen to the gulls as they wheel overhead in the azure-blue,

cloudless sky, and to the waves gently lapping the shore. Get the feeling in your body of peace and contentment. Enjoy it for as long as you can.

2. Garden

Imagine that you are strolling in a beautiful garden. What different types of flowers and shrubs can you see? You sit down on the lawn by a pretty little fishpond and see the goldfish swimming lazily around in it. You admire the graceful water-lilies, and the dragonflies flitting around them with rainbow-colored wings. The only sounds you can hear are the buzzing of a bumble bee and the faint drone of a plane high overhead, which seems to heighten the peace and tranquility of the scene. Enjoy your garden for as long as you can.

With visualizations of this sort you need to come back gently to reality to avoid feeling jarred. So when you have finished, open your eyes, look round, remind yourself of where you are and spend a few minutes reminding yourself what you have to do next.

Chapter 9

Breaking Free to Love Yourself

Codependency and loving yourself

IT IS PARTICULARLY IMPORTANT FOR ANY-body who has any responsibility for others (and this means nearly everybody) to ensure that they are looking after themselves at least as well as they are looking after the people in their care. This applies to parents, especially to single parents, and those who have taken on responsibility for the aged, a widowed mother, perhaps, or anyone in a caring profession. The danger is that you can start living for them first, rather than for yourself, and lose touch with your own needs, including the need to love yourself.

Recent research has led to the coining of a new term, codependency, to describe this destructive pattern. We have long been aware of how the families of addicts, with the best will in the world, can in fact perpetuate the addiction: wives or husbands continually clean up after their spouse's latest binge and then hide the booze, feeling it is their duty to be supportive all the time, however badly they, their friends or their children are treated. Many battered wives come back for more abuse or violence time and time again. Parents feel they always have to be "there" for adolescents hooked on heroin, come what may. All these people are "codependents," which means that they are very much better at taking responsibility for other people's happiness than creating their own.

Codependents are also addicts: addicted to sacrificing their own lives for somebody else. They are at a loss if they do not have somebody to look after. This provides meaning to their lives, and they collect such people, over and over again. They *need* to be needed. And playing the role of the "rescuer" gives them an identity and a reason for living. In relationships codependents zone in on the "lame ducks," and are ready to put up with anything: poverty, drunkenness, invalidation and abuse or infidelity.

Denial that anything is wrong is very much a part of codependency. The pretense of "happy families," presenting a façade of normality, continually excusing bad behavior at home and a misplaced, desperate optimism that everything is going to be "all right" are the hallmarks of a family in which codependent ways of relating were and are the norm. And it is in such families, particularly when there is an alcoholic in the family, that codependents are developed. Its members learn over the years not to talk, not to feel and not to trust. What hope have they of loving themselves growing up in such an atmosphere?

Codependency is extremely widespread—most of us are codependent to some degree—probably because it masquerades as true caring and is approved of in our culture. Women are particularly vulnerable to becoming codependent on their husbands. We have all met the "little woman" who seems to have no existence apart from through her husband. She spends all her time ensuring that he is comfortable, fed and sexually satisfied. She may have given up her own ambitions or sacrificed her own career so as to be more available to him. As the years go by she loses more and more the sense of her own identity and loses touch with her own needs. But the payoff is her satisfaction in being a "good wife," and the approval of her friends. And, if she is deserted by her partner (as she might well be, for codependency makes people *boring*), she is secure in the position of the blameless wife who "did everything for her husband."

But men can also get "hooked" into making others the center of their lives. The dedicated doctor or therapist who feels he has to be "there" for his patients day or night, the business man who cannot ease up before he gives himself a coronary and whose home life comes very much second to negotiating the next deal, these men have traded labels like being a "good doctor" or "successful" and the admiration of others for quality of life. They have been taken over by something outside themselves, forgetting that "What shall it profit a man, if he shall gain the whole world and lose his own soul?" (Mark, 8.36).

Codependents are people who have to depend on others for their own sense of worth and self-esteem. They cannot love themselves for who they are and have to lose touch with their own feelings and sense of who they are. The consequent inner emptiness can lead to alienation, a sense of being "unreal," and of not being "in" what one is saying, feeling or doing. This can bring in its train depression, illness and compulsive behavior such as drinking, gambling, promiscuity, religious mania.

Most of us have elements of codependency in the ways we relate. Very few people are so in touch with themselves that they manage to achieve complete independence of others, or non-identification from their roles and relationships. Try answering the following questions to get some idea of how codependent you are.

How codependent are you?

YES NO

- Do you often feel frightened and nervous of other people?
- If you see a fight in the street, does your heart beat faster, as if somehow you are responsible for it?
- Do you constantly need approval from other people?
- Do angry people frighten you?
- Do you get very upset by personal criticism?
- Do you feel responsible for the other people in your life?

- Do you ever feel your family would fall apart without you?
- Do you ever feel guilty when you stand up for yourself instead of giving in to the wishes of others?
- Do you find it hard to refuse a request for help?
- Do you tend to attract people who seem to need a lot of help?
- Would you call yourself a perfectionist?
- Do you tend to be your own sternest critic?
- Do you seem to come alive in a crisis?
- Do other people see you as one who copes wonderfully?
- Do you ever feel that other people do not appreciate all you do for them?
- Do you ever feel that people tend to abandon you through no fault of your own?
- Would you call yourself a very loyal person?
- Do you find it difficult to have fun?
- Do you always try to avoid conflict instead of facing up to it?
- Do you ever feel you could have been more successful if other people hadn't got in your way?

(From *Codependency* by David Stafford and Liz Hodgkinson, Piatkus 1991.)

The more yes answers you have on your list, the more likely you are to be codependent. Don't make this yet another reason for beating yourself up, because *everybody* is codependent to some extent and the world would be a nightmarish jungle if nobody cared for anybody else. It becomes a problem only when we "go over the top" with our loyalty and lose touch with ourselves and what we need. Ask a true codependent what they are in touch with, needing, or what they want to do next, and the answer is usually a blank. They are not used to considering what is right for *them*, and feel they have no choice. Not surprisingly they find it difficult to relax and have fun. They are addicted to playing the "responsible citizen" or "caring person," carrying on into adult life the role of "Mummy's little helper" in which they cast themselves early in life. They were not to realize that this role would prove a life sentence of alienation from themselves.

Dealing with codependency

Fortunately, it is possible to reverse codependent patterns. What is needed is more awareness, either through really examining your life on your own and deciding that you have been a doormat for too long, or working with a counselor or in therapy, individual or group.

The important thing is to recognize the patterns in yourself, to find the Pleaser in you (see Chapter 4), and understand why things are as they are. Then set about tackling this condition in a positive way. Whatever you do, remember to be good to yourself. It cannot be selfish or uncaring to find out what you need and then to set about fulfilling it. If you always wanted to learn to play golf, for example, do it! And as you get better at pleasing yourself you will begin to respect yourself, and as you respect yourself you will find that others respect you.

Don't try to be what others want you to be. Resist such attempts to control you. And resist trying to control other people's lives. The key to freedom from codependency is to learn to choose for yourself, and to say "No" when you want to.

Don't expect other people to approve of your newfound capacity for choice initially, or for daring to say "No, enough is enough." They have as much invested in you staying as you are, as you have invested in rescuing them. You might have to change your partner, or your job, but freedom always has its price. As long as you are locked in codependency, your partner will not get better. He or she doesn't need to. They have you.

Breaking patterns

One of the signs that you are beginning to love yourself more is when you stop continually *blaming* yourself for your "defects" and shortcomings, and instead become interested in *understanding* why you behave the way you do. You need to become interested in your own process, in what makes you "tick," what "pushes your buttons" and why, instead of continually judging yourself. From blaming and judging yourself all you will get is depression and lack of self-esteem. There is no growth. However, when you start to "treat yourself as you would your best friend," i.e. with goodwill, understanding, forgiveness and compassion, you get to see how, given your core ideas, your behavior is totally appropriate.

In this sense you are always "right."

What we call "faults" are merely unawareness and chronic maladaptive behavior. If you want to change your behavior so you can approve of yourself more you need to become more self-aware and watch out for your habitual, automatic ways of reacting. And when you catch yourself "in the act," try doing something different for a change, deliberately, and with choice. For example, decide deliberately not to do something you've always done through duty—make yourself say "No." It can feel scary to try something new, for you are on unfamiliar ground. But it is worth taking risks; you will gain in confidence, and you will certainly feel a lot freer. The more you are *willing* to break your fixed patterns of thinking and behavior—especially self-limiting and negative ones—the lighter and more autonomous you will become.

A very good way to get wise as to *which* patterns you are "stuck" in is to find a good therapy group. There are many such groups to choose from, e.g. women's groups, Gestalt groups, Transactional Analysis, "Twelve Step" groups such as CoDa, and so on. The members of the group will make you realize when you are "trotting out the same old numbers," i.e., repeating your pattern, and support you. To be a participant in a good group is a powerful experience, and will help you grow as perhaps nothing else can.

If you don't like the idea of joining a group, discover the value of talking to your friends, your partner, or anyone you feel you can trust. Don't suppress your feelings. Look into them and learn from them.

Talk them over, and talk about who you really are and what you need to restore or build your self-esteem.

Start to value yourself
One of the most important patterns to break is either invalidating yourself, or putting yourself down, or limiting yourself in any way. Remember that we create our future from moment to moment by what we think and say. It is as if the Universe is listening to us and is totally prepared to accept us at our own self-valuation. So when we say things like "Just my luck," or "This always happens to me," "Life is hard" or "People are so unkind," we are asking for experiences like that to prove that we are right. And they will come. So, whenever you catch yourself doing this, immediately cancel out the negative statement with an affirmation to the contrary. For suitable affirmations, see page 94.

It is equally important never to allow other people's negative thoughts or invalidations of you in either. This will only hammer more nails into the coffin of your self-esteem. Others will often generalize about "the way it is" in a negative way, and include us in their pessimism. "We all feel like this, don't we?" or "It's a bitch of a life, isn't it?" or something similar. Never let such comments pass without jumping in straightaway with something like, "Well, that's not my reality" or, "No, I think life is beautiful."

Affirmations need to be *actualized* in real-life situations if the seeds you have planted in your subconscious are to flourish. In other words, you have to start behaving as if they are already the case. For example, if your affirmation is for radiant health, then to drag yourself around and to tell everybody who asks (or who doesn't) how awful you are feeling is a castration of the new energy that is trying to come through in your life. Rather, choose to ignore the aches and pains, the breathlessness or low energy, and start acting as if you were already healed. "Put on a happy face," like Norman Cousins (see Chapter 6). *Act* healthy. Acting "as if" is a powerful mood changer and, as we have suggested, also has the power to affect our body. Similarly, if your affirmation has been for more confidence, help it to manifest by *acting* confident, even if you really feel like shrinking into the woodwork. Open up your body posture, breathe freely, smile, put some power into your voice.

I know an American "New Age" therapist, now very successful, who was once hard up and desperate for clients. She was therefore thrilled to get a call from a radio producer who wanted to feature her regularly on a phone-in service for listeners. He promised to contact her as soon as he had finalized the format of the program, which he said would be in a week or so. He didn't. She went through agonies waiting for the phone to ring, and got angry with the producer, and as she put it to me in the Californian jargon, felt "ripped off." Eventually, months later, when she had given up ever hearing anything more, the producer rang again to give her the dates when she would be "on." To his amazement, she told him she no longer wanted to do the programs. He reminded her that the program would be aired at a prime time, how many people would be listening to her, what this would do for her career etc. To this she replied that she had decided that feeling good about herself was infinitely more important to her than the chance of fame or fortune. She told him that she felt he had treated her with disrespect in not contacting her sooner, as promised, which made her feel like a commodity to be exploited. She did not feel valued as a person, and declined to see herself in the role of a suppliant, a beggar.

The interesting thing is that, soon after, she was approached by a leading publisher to write a book on her approach to personal growth. The book has since become a bestseller. She now has more clients than she can handle, and is in great demand for therapy groups and public lectures all over the western United States and Europe. Her explanation of this is that she had learned that when she comes from a place of need, of desperation, nothing ever works out.

Control your subpersonalities

Keeping a sharp eye on our subpersonalities is very important if they are not to run away with us and control our lives. The Workaholic, the Pleaser, the needy Child are all OK in their place, but when they clamor for our attention regardless of appropriateness or the needs of the moment (for which they care not a scrap) we could be in trouble. We feel driven to slave away even when there is no need, do things we don't want to do, never say "No" for fear of upsetting others, irritate our lovers by our constant clamoring for attention, possessiveness or need for reassurance. The most virulent part of us is our Internal Critic, who never lets up reminding us of our shortcomings and "how we should be." Listen to your subpersonalities, but don't let them "pull your strings." *You* are the boss. Stay in charge, and choose which energies you want to bring out, and when.

As we saw in Chapter 4, in relating to people, rather than reacting blindly to their words or behavior, try to sense the place they are coming from. Often, hidden behind the angry words and blaming, is the Inner Child who feels insecure and unloved. If you can address the Child directly and ask it what it needs to feel good again, you can bypass the verbal ping-pong and need to defend and justify yourself that figures so largely in many relationship quarrels. Similarly, if you can stop yourself from reacting like a rebellious Son or Daughter when your partner is coming on like a Controlling Parent, you will save a lot of energy and be in a better position to stand up for yourself. The biggest patterns to change are those of blaming, and playing victim. Unless you drop these you will always be giving your power away to other people.

Trust in abundance

If you want prosperity, you have to develop prosperity consciousness (see Chapter 10). Break the pattern of seeing yourself as a beggar, continually hassling for money, worrying about bills, comparing yourself with others who have more than you and getting depressed about your "failure" to make it in the world. The more you dwell on what you don't have, the poorer you will get. You will attract the experiences that go with a feeling of *lack*. Rather, remind yourself of what you have already and be grateful for it. And if you *have* to compare, then choose to compare yourself with those who are worse off than you—and there are certainly plenty of those in the world today. Trust in the Abundance of the Universe: "Ask and you shall receive." Miracles happen when you trust.

I remember once sharing a flat with a friend who was a bit of a hippy and refused to be bothered about money. It was "uncool." I was nagging him one day about an electricity bill that had to be paid urgently. His share of it was £36 (it was a long time ago!). In my panic I saw the electricity board cutting off our supply of heating in the middle of winter, and was furious when he refused to get as rattled as I was. "It'll come," he said. "Trust." And to my amazement, come it did. A check from the Inland Revenue for tax overpaid arrived—and, incredibly, it was for exactly £36! This is a true story and, in the jargon we loved to use in those days, it "blew my mind."

Affirmations for breaking free to love yourself

I am not my mother. I do not have her thoughts and feelings.

I am not my father. I do not have his thoughts and feelings.

I am not my teachers. I do not limit myself by what they taught me.

I am not limited by my early religious education.

I am not here to meet the expectations of others.

I can say "No"—and feel good about it.

I now settle only for what I want, not just for what I can get.

I trust in the Abundance of the Universe.

I trust that I shall receive whatever I need.

I have forgiven anyone that I mistakenly thought ever hurt me.

I love and approve of myself every moment.

People love me for being who I am.

Strangers are friends to be.

I feel confident that I can handle any situation that arises.

I am able to defend myself against any attack.

Fear is a thing of the past.

I forgive my parents totally. They were doing the best they could.

I am grateful for all the good things life brings to me every day.

I now do only the things I feel like doing.

It's OK to express myself any way I choose.

The more I look after myself, the happier other people are.

Visualization for breaking free to love yourself

Let your mind wander back over your life so far. Remember all the good times, and also things that you regret and which cause you pain. See them in as much detail as possible. Now bundle all these memories into a sack and tie it up. Dispose of the sack in any way that feels right to you. For example, you could burn it, or throw it into a river and watch it sink below the surface.

Be really whole, and all things
will come to you
—*Tao Te Ching, 2*

Chapter 10

Prosperity Consciousness

Feeling rich is not being rich

SO MANY PEOPLE FEEL UNCOMFORTABLE about money, and as it can be a cause of depression and much unhappiness I want to say a few words about it here. Whether you have a lot of money or only a little, you can feel good about it and good about yourself. But if you have a bad relationship with money it can make you feel inadequate, always controlled by the lack of it or the surfeit of it or the insatiable desire for more.

Prosperity consciousness is not about *being* rich, but about *feeling* rich. One can have all the money in the world, and still *feel* a pauper. Likewise, if you have a healthy attitude to money you can have very little and enjoy your life to the full. If we are to accept ourselves for who we are and love ourselves unconditionally we have to feel abundant and appreciate what we have.

Let me tell you about a friend of mine, whom we shall call Martin. We first met in an ongoing therapy group way back in the early 1970s in London and immediately got on well together. I was attracted by his charm and diffidence that bordered on self-deprecation, but above all by his sense of humour, especially when talking about himself. Often the group would fall about laughing at the droll way he would describe events in his past, some of them quite heavy.

I did not know at first just how wealthy he was, for we all wore the "comfortable clothes" which were *de rigueur* in therapy groups, jeans, sweatshirts etc., in all, a sloppy lot. The first inkling I had that there was a millionaire in our midst was when the group traipsed up to Yorkshire to do a weekend group "at his place up north," as he put it. This turned out to be his family home, with wisteria climbing all over the mellow, red-brick walls, and set amid rolling lawns and flowerbeds, and one of the most delightful places I had ever seen. Inside the house were antiques, and on the walls spotlit oil paintings that we learned later were of his ancestors who had owned the estate for centuries.

I later learned that Martin owned an apartment block just around the corner from Harrods, and lived in the penthouse flat when he was in London. This was not that often, however, for he spent the summer months in the Auvergne, where he owned property and vineyards.

It was while I was driving through France that

he invited us to stop over for a few days before continuing our drive down to the Pyrenees. As usual he was the perfect host, a fund of information about the history of the place, delivered with his usual modesty and wit.

The night before we left we were all sitting in the garden enjoying a gastronomic dinner *al fresco*, washed down with his excellent, home-grown claret. It was a balmy night in August and we reminisced, about the therapy group and other things, until well into the small hours. At one point, rather indiscreetly perhaps, I remarked to him how marvelous it must be to be so wealthy, and not to have to worry about money like us ordinary mortals. To my amazement he told me that he never *stopped* worrying about money, not about how to pay the bills perhaps, but about his investments, the responsibility he felt he had to preserve the family fortunes, the ill-advised business projects that had lessened his confidence in his own financial acumen, fluctuations in the stock market . . . I have never forgotten that conversation since, and call it to mind whenever I start getting discontented about my own non-millionaire status.

Money is not the only form of wealth. Good health, peace of mind and loving relationships are riches that we often take for granted if we are fortunate enough to have them. And, especially, if we come from a rich family background, we can take having money so much for granted that we don't actually appreciate it.

Another friend of mine is also very wealthy, but is one of the unhappiest people I know. She is lonely, makes disastrous choices in men and is plagued by chronic ill-health.

At the other end of the scale one sees people who have literally nothing, and yet seem to enjoy their lives fully. When I was living in India the kitchen window of my flat overlooked one of the many shanty towns. The poor who come into the cities from the villages build themselves ramshackle dwellings from whatever materials they can find: corrugated iron, cardboard and so forth. Every bit of space is used up by the families who live there. These people have nothing in the way of worldly goods, apart from a few brass cooking pots and the clothes they stand up in.

Since I am an early riser I would often observe, as I ate my breakfast, the little community slowly coming to life again in the bright morning sunshine. What always struck me was the calm *dignity* of these people as they performed their morning chores, fetching water, washing their pots, getting ready for what would be for many of them a day of begging. The women squatted barefoot in their brightly-colored saris, cooking over the fire, or getting the children (of which there were a horde) ready, plaiting their hair and applying make-up to their eyes. Poor as they were, they obviously took pride in their appearance and looked like princesses, one and all. They seemed a happy lot, chattering away to each other and to the children playing in the sun. There was a lot of laughter. Compared to them, we travelers from the West were millionaires, but we certainly didn't seem to be having as good a time as they were. Wealth is relative. Having a lot

is not as important as being able to enjoy what you
do have.

Money is energy

Like everything else, the energy that is money follows certain laws. The amount of money we attract
to ourselves is related to where we ourselves are "at"
and our level of self-esteem—whether we think we
deserve it, our expectations and our assumptions
about it. If we *enjoy* what we do, we will usually
get the money we need. Money will not be the most
important thing in our lives. But the more poverty
conscious we allow ourselves to get, the more we
shall experience ourselves as beggars.

Recent research from America suggests that everybody has a subconscious limit to the amount of
money they feel comfortable with. If they go beyond
their self-imposed limit, they get rid of the sur-
plus. It just seems to "go through their fingers":
they cannot seem to hold on to it. They may
be promoted, earn more and still the total on
their bank statement at the end of the month is
about the same. Since, as we have postulated, the
experiences that we get "from the outside" always
match the patterns we carry in our heads, a common experience (certainly true in my own case)
is that as soon as one settles back with a sigh
of relief that the bank loan (or the car, or the
mortgage) has been paid off, through the letter
box comes an unwelcome surprise in the form of
a crunching demand for something else that has to
be paid for!

Assumptions about money

Very few people are balanced when it comes to dealing with money. Either we are greedy for it, hoard it or "blow" it, are embarrassed by having it or depressed by not having it. Talking about it is "bad form" in civilised circles and almost as taboo as talking about death. Money is power, probably the biggest source of power in the world. It "talks." It can control our lives, one way or the other. Very few people are masters of money: usually they are slaves to it.

Check up on your relationship to money by answering the following questions.

YES NO

- Do you worry constantly about your financial situation?
- Do you feel that all your problems would be solved if you had more money?
- Do you measure your success by the amount of money you have?
- Do you think that money is the "root of all evil?"
- Do you think that it "makes the world go round?"
- Do you think that the wrong people have it?
- Do you think that you deserve to be rich?
- Are you convinced that *you* will never be rich?
- Do you find it uncomfortable to have to talk about money?

- Do you feel that the amount of money in the world is limited, and that if you had more, others would have to go without?
- Do you shrink from having to negotiate a fee for your services?
- Do you find it hard to ask for money owing to you?
- Do you panic when you receive a bill you can't pay?

How many times did you answer "Yes?"

As we have seen, since our energy is always constellated according to a specific pattern, it goes on attracting the same sort of experiences until we change that pattern. In other words, *change the inner and the outer follows*. So don't allow yourself to slither deeper into poverty consciousness by constantly worrying about money. It will only make matters worse than they are. Stop thinking like a beggar. Instead, train your mind to think like an emperor. Instead of constantly telling yourself things like, "I can't afford this," and complaining to your friends about the price of everything, put your energy into creating a new reality for yourself based on trust in the Abundance in the Universe—and your birthright to your rightful share in it.

At the end of this chapter you will find affirmations to help you change your set ideas about money and program your subconscious in new, more positive ways. Encourage the development of prosperity consciousness by actualizing these affirmations in real-life situations. In other words, act as if you *believed in them, as if they were already the case*. For a change, take a taxi, rather than queuing for a bus in pouring rain—and tip well. Feel good about it. Drop the pattern when shopping of always looking for the cheapest. It you can, go for quality instead, whether in food or in clothes. You deserve the best. Give it to yourself. If you value yourself, others will value you too. You will feel abundant and attract abundance.

Money follows the project

It has long been my suspicion that the Universe does not understand money. It responds to creativity, it responds to need. But when, in our panic, we ask it for more cash so that we can feel safer, the cosmic computer registers a blank. It seems to be more interested in what you want money *for*, rather than in increasing the numbers printed on your bank statement just so you can feel better.

Think of Mother Teresa and how she operates. With no money of her own she produces, out of nowhere, the substantial sums needed for her projects. Wealthy people queue up to support her charitable work and feel privileged to do so. She doesn't beg, she prays—and trusts.

The importance of focusing on a goal
The clearer you are about the project you want to create, the more your clarity acts like a magnet to attract support from the environment for that project. Visualize yourself doing it, and visualize people reacting positively to it, needing it or buying

it. Focusing precisely on the goal sets the process in motion. (You are more likely to score a goal in a game of football if you center yourself and take focused aim than just kicking out at random.)

Don't specify *how* money is going to come for your project. Leave that up to your Guardian Angel, or fate or whatever else you believe in. Angels and the fates don't like to be limited in this way. If you are clear, and trust, and nobody else is going to be damaged by what you want to create, be sure that it will manifest, sooner or later, perhaps in a way you could not have yourself conceived. Be realistic, plan for a miracle!

If you want to start a project which you really believe in, and you need money to get yourself started, then I suggest you try the Creative Law technique on page 136. But don't be greedy! You will only get what you really need. If you want to establish a better relationship with money, and yourself, read *Creating Abundance* by Andrew Ferguson (Piatkus 1992).

Affirmations for prosperity consciousness

Money comes to me freely; I do not have to hassle for it.

I always have as much money as I need.

Being prosperous feels perfectly SAFE.

I am the master of money.

Money is my servant.

Others are happy at my good fortune.

I trust in the Abundance of the Universe.

I enjoy treating myself and others.

Visualizations for prosperity consciousness

Imagine you have become rich, perhaps from good fortune, or through the success of your projects.

Feel in your body how nice it is never again to have to worry about money. Enjoy this feeling for as long as you can.

Now visualize to what purposes you will put your wealth. How, for example, will you treat yourself and with whom will you share your good fortune? Be specific. See in detail the places you will visit, the things you will buy and the joy that you are now able to bring to the people you love.

Chapter 11

Staying in Charge
of Your Life

Acknowledge your power

I WOULD GUESS THAT A FAIR PROPORTION OF
the readers who bought this book did so because
they felt they would like to have more confidence
in themselves. And I can understand this perfectly,
having in my younger days been crippled by shyness
and self-doubt. This is not to say that sometimes I
don't *still* feel shy, or unsure on occasion. The difference now is that I am more willing to allow myself
to feel the way I do without making it a problem. In
other words, I can *acknowledge* how I am feeling and
allow it to stay there.

There is a big difference between, for example,
having butterflies before an examination or speaking in public, and having expectations that if you
don't give the performance of your life you are a

Useless Person. It is having expectations of oneself that are too high that in fact create the tension that we experience as lack of confidence. The more "perfect" we think we should be, the less freely our energy flows into what we are doing.

Curiously enough, people are afraid to acknowledge their own power. The word has unpleasant associations in our minds. We think of "power-hungry" politicians and their destructiveness, exploitation and manipulation of others. Perhaps above all, we associate it with being selfish, egotistical and uncaring of others. Deeply ingrained in us is the fear of our own power, stemming from our fantasies as children about our own omnipotence and our fear of draining our mother with our demands and therefore killing her. And, as we grew up, conformity and deference to authority seemed the best way to keep out of trouble.

And yet the truth is that we *are* powerful—all of us. We are told in the Bible that we were made in the image of God—and there aren't many beings more powerful than God! We are creative, self-determining beings with the power to take charge of our lives and to sculpture them as we will.

But we are a bit like the tiger who had the mistaken idea that he was a sheep. He thought like a sheep, behaved like a sheep, lived with sheep. One day he was wakened to his true identity by an old tiger who made him look at his own reflection in a river. The effect on the pseudo-sheep was dramatic, akin to an enlightenment experience. Seeing at last who he really was, his whole being changed. He let out a mighty roar and henceforth actualized the

powerful, beautiful creature that he really was—
and had been all the time without knowing it.

Taking responsibility

What, then, do we mean by "power?" It simply
means knowing who you really are, rather than
being conditioned as to how you think you should
be. It means being centered in yourself and in touch
with what you want—and giving yourself permission
to go for it. It means trusting your own strength to
achieve what you want to achieve, and your capacity to respond appropriately to whatever challenges
life throws in your way. Above all, it means never
seeing yourself as a victim. And it is by meeting
these challenges, one after the other, that trust
in our own power—call it self-confidence if you
will—is developed in us. But most often we call
these challenges "problems" and wish they weren't
there. We worry and panic, and try to slither off the
hook, unaware that the "way out" is always the "way
through."

When we react rather than respond, we place
ourselves in the position of being "at effect" rather
than "at cause." By this we mean that we become
victims, and therefore experience the things that
go with victim-consciousness: desperation, *Angst*,
resentment, stress, feelings of "Why me?," and often
"Poor me." The list of things we can feel victimized
by can be endless, from illness to poverty, from
employers to lovers, even, for some people, a phenomenon over which we have no control, like the
weather.

The essence of being a victim is the sense that we don't have any choice. There is a special victim vocabulary which includes phrases like, "I couldn't do anything else," "You [They] made me do it" and so forth. Whenever, for example, we say to our partner "You make me feel good [bad, inadequate or whatever]," we give our power of self-determination away and cast ourselves in the role of victim. For nobody else has the power to make us feel anything. Our feelings are our feelings. To claim anything else is a manipulation, aimed usually at making the other feel guilty or sorry for us. In other words, we choose to play weak.

As well as giving ourselves *choice*, non-victim status is very much to do with taking responsibility for our own experience. You must acknowledge (hard as it can undoubtedly be sometimes) that in some way you have created this situation yourself and ask yourself "Now what am I going to do about it?" Straightaway, you are back in charge, and have taken back your power. What we create, we can uncreate. But first we have to be willing to accept responsibility for our own creations.

My own experience is that acknowledging that *I* created this mess is somehow a relief and is actually empowering. There is no one to blame. It is also important not to blame yourself. So you may have been unaware, or made unfortunate choices in the past, but how else are you going to learn to be more aware, or to make better choices in the future? It is no accident that you are having to wade through these particular difficulties at this time. Every happening contains a lesson for you to learn, and you may as well learn it now. If you shirk it, life has a way of coming back at you with something even more heavy and difficult until you get the message. It is important to realize that we are not put in this world to be more *comfortable*, but to become more *conscious*.

Gerald Jampolsky suggests that there are certain words and phrases that serve to limit our power. Watch out for them. They are:

impossible

can't

try

limitation

if only

but

however

difficult

ought to

should

doubt

(and any words that place you or anyone else in a category, any words that tend to measure or evaluate you or other people,

any words that tend to judge or condemn you or someone else).

(From *Love is Letting Go of Fear* by Gerald G. Jampolsky. Reprinted by permission of Celestial Arts, Berkeley, Calif.).

Fritz Perls, founder of Gestalt Therapy, used to insist that his clients exchange the word "but" for "and." "But" cancels out a statement, whereas "and" enlarges upon it. Often our feelings are mixed: for example, "I do love you *and* sometimes you can be a pain in the neck."

Similarly, using "can't" suggests our powerlessness in a particular situation, whereas "won't" expresses that we have a choice.

Knowing what you want

A big part of being centered, feeling "at source" and in charge of your life is knowing what you want—and what you don't want. And if you are clear about what you want, it is so much easier to get it. You don't fritter away your energy in confusion and double messages. You simply ask for it directly, to make it happen. But first you have to believe that it's OK for you to get what you want, so long as other people are not damaged by your desire. The ideas that castrate us in our search for fulfillment are that other people won't like us if we are "selfish," or that our gain is another's loss.

For example, poverty consciousness, which we looked at in Chapter 10, goes very much with being a victim. The truth is that there is enough to go round, that the Universe is Abundant, and that looking after yourself, far from being anti-social, relieves other people of feeling obliged to do it for you.

It is important to be able to say "No," and mean it, when necessary, just as it is important to be able also to give a full-hearted "Yes," when you want to. If we are yea-sayers all the time, afraid to say "No," we cannot set any boundaries (see Chapter 8). Some people may not like us for it. But at least they will respect us, and know that they can trust we mean "Yes" when it comes.

Our need for unconditional love

Ultimately we have to learn to give to ourselves what we need. And everybody's basic need is to be able to love themselves, and to feel accepted and loved unconditionally. Nothing else satisfies. But before we can do this there is work to be done on clearing the backlog of emotions, "personal baggage" from the past, that makes us feel that we are unlovable, that it is not OK to feel good about ourselves—and all that rubbish.

The truth is, that even if we do get love offered to us, unless we have got into the habit of loving ourselves, either we won't notice we are loved, or won't believe it and won't let it in. Loving yourself is very much a do-it-yourself-first business.

It is good just to ask yourself from time to time *why* you are not getting what you need. Using the model of the outside world mirroring where you are at will often give you a clue as to how you are stopping things coming to you. Remember that we get back what we put out, multiplied. So, for example, if you feel you need more love in your life, be more loving yourself. Treat your partner with more gentleness and consideration, instead of taking them for granted. Smile more, show more interest in other people, and they are likely to show more interest in you. And above all, stop judging and comparing. Instead, try to understand the place where people who offend you with their behavior are coming from. They, like you, are only doing what they feel impelled to do to make themselves feel better.

We are all in the same boat. Choosing to put out more love is a decision you will never regret. Decide when you wake up each morning to be as loving as you can in the course of this day. Having this intention in your subconscious will sweeten your day, make difficulties evaporate and attract small miracles. Nothing works like love.

Getting your needs met

Being in charge of your life means that you can recognize your needs and fulfill them. This involves learning to manipulate the environment, rather than manipulating other people. It also involves becoming more aware of your own process and tuning in to what your needs actually are.

Think about the subpersonalities we looked at in Chapter 4. It would be safe to say that it is the Child part of us that first feels need. Unfortunately, our Inner Child is not very articulate in expressing need: it is likely merely to feel unsatisfied, that it wants *something*, without knowing what it is. It is therefore likely to nag us, to clamor for attention, to complain, and be petulant and fractious, just like a real child. Subjectively, we are likely to experience this as restlessness, depression, bleakness or irritability. How can we be in charge if we don't know what we want?

It is primarily the function of our Inner Parent to protect our Inner Child's welfare and interests and see it gets nourished. Those of us who were fortunate enough to have parents who were caring, consistent and, above all, *there*, will have introjected this into our own personalities and will have developed a supportive and capable Inner Parent. But if our real-life parents were too strict, withholding or absent, it will be that much harder for our Inner Child to feel truly *held* and fulfilled.

Becoming clear about what you need, and risking asking for it directly, are the first rules for getting your needs met. Maybe you will, and maybe you won't. But, at least, having the courage to ask for it is an exercise in self-validation and will strengthen your sense of self. As Matthew (7.7) says "Ask, and it shall be given you." Don't assume other people automatically will know what you need: usually they don't.

Assertion versus aggression

When you have decided what to ask for, remember that there is a difference between being assertive and being aggressive. We tend to ask for something in an aggressive way if we think either that we are not going to get it, or feel that we don't really deserve to get it. The effect on the other person is usually negative, for nobody likes to be pressurized or harangued. You are more likely to get what you want if the energy you put into your request is firm and dignified and you are coming from a position of "Of course I deserve to have this." You feel in charge of your life and of your needs.

Needs and wants

We will always get what we need. We may not always get what we want. We are a part of the Whole that brought us into existence because It wanted us to be here. It nourishes and sustains us. If It hadn't, we would not still be here. It hears our needs (and our supplication in prayer), but It is not very interested in our ego-trips about money and power.

The difference between needing and wanting is akin to the difference between merely having a preference or being addicted. You stay in charge when you seek to fill a need, or express a preference. Wants and addictions, on the other hand, drag you along by the scruff of the neck. The more you get, the more you must have.

One of the effects of our "consumer society" and the relentless advertising that goes with it is that we can get confused as to what we really need. Do we really *need* that new washing machine (car, three-piece suite, carpet) we saw on the telly last night? Or would having it merely make us feel smug about ourselves, that we have as much as the neighbors? If so, this is only another example of what we talked about in Chapter 6 where we looked at "filling the gap," our inner emptiness, by stuffing ourselves with goodies.

The Creative Law

Once you are clear as to what you really need, as opposed to merely what you want, set the universal wheels in motion by "vibing" or "putting out" for it. One of the ways of doing this is by using the Creative Law. This is a structure that shows you, step by step, how to attract the things you need to you. More than anything else, the Creative Law is a device for getting you yourself to take responsibility for filling your own needs and to trust that you can in fact do this.

Silva mind trainers (who use a form of mind control invented by José Silva) recommend you take the following steps in order to speed up the process of things coming to you that you have asked for. You need:

1. a clear intention;

2. faith that it is on its way already;

3. intense expectation;

4. gratitude when it manifests.

Try it out for yourself. In our example we are imagining that you need a new flat, but you can adapt the steps to apply to anything you *really* need.

Stage 1

Decide *exactly* what you want to manifest in your life. Be as detailed as possible, and fix a time limit within which you want it to happen. For example, if you need a new flat, decide how many rooms you will need, which area it will be in, which floor it will be on, whether there will be a garden etc. See the place in your imagination, in as much detail as you can. Don't forget the price range, or you may be offered the flat you want, but at a price you cannot afford. Be clear that you really want whatever it is, for it will surely manifest, and then you may be stuck with it. Remember than once something has manifested on the material plane it is harder to "uncreate" it again. Do not specify *how* it will come—leave that up to your Guardian Angel, or the fates or whoever (and be prepared for surprises!). Above all, ensure that nobody else will be harmed or suffer from the realization of your creation.

Stage 2
Imagine you are listening to a conversation between two of your friends in which they are discussing your good fortune and success. What exactly are they saying?

Stage 3
Imagine *yourself* breaking the good news to somebody else and receiving their congratulations.

Stage 4
Get the feeling in your body that your new flat has in fact already materialized. See yourself already installed and experience how good that feels.

Stage 5
Express your gratitude to the Universe for meeting your needs.

Stage 6
When you feel finished and the energy starts to go out of your visualization, put your new flat into a balloon and watch it float away.

Stage 7
From now on assume that it is only a matter of time before your mind creation manifests on the material plane. For example, start checking removals firms

in the *Yellow Pages*, getting estimates, deciding on color schemes etc.

Don't brag about what you have done to others. The Creative Law is not an ego-trip. It is more like a prayer. We all have the power to create, and we are doing it all the time. But some people disclaim responsibility for their creations, for good or ill.

Affirmations for staying in charge

I have the power to create what I will for myself.

I am a powerful, capable, creative and successful being.

I have total confidence in my own abilities.

People love and respect me for being strong and knowing what I want.

I can, and I will.

It's OK for me to get what I want.

I deserve to experience satisfaction in my life.

It's OK for me to say "No."

I now win all the time.

Everything I touch is a success.

Feeling in charge of my life feels totally SAFE.

Visualizations for staying in charge

Conquering anxiety

(Use this visualization when you are anxious about your forthcoming performance, e.g. taking an examination, being interviewed for a new job, public speaking etc.).

Visualize yourself giving the performance in as much detail as you can, e.g. sitting at your desk in the examination hall, reading the question paper, or sitting opposite your interviewer. What words are being said, and what questions asked? Get the feeling in your body of total confidence, of satisfaction that everything is going very well. You are being asked questions that you take in your stride, or delivering an elegant and witty speech you can see from the audience's reaction and laughter that they are really enjoying.

Finish the visualization by seeing in your mind the results of your performance, e.g. receiving your examination results (a distinction of course!), your new employer's letter inviting you to start working for them, and setting out work terms and salary (more than you expected), or receiving compliments for your speech. And don't forget to compliment *yourself* for doing a good job.

Gaining clarity

(Use this visualization for clarity when you have some decision to make.)

Imagine yourself out in the countryside. It is a clear, beautiful, sunny day. You walk through a meadow and cross a stream via an old wooden bridge. You are heading for the hut where an old woman lives whom your friends have told you is immensely wise and can help you with your problems.

Eventually you espy the hut, nestling in a hollow by the banks of the stream. The door is open. You go in and see an old lady sitting in a rocking chair. She has a kind face and you sense that she has vast experience of the ways of the world. She has been expecting you, and greets you as if she already knows you. You feel you have met her somewhere before, and instinctively feel that you can trust her guidance.

She ask's "What is your question?" and you tell her. What is her answer?

Epilogue

Being Who We Really Are

WHENEVER I TALK ABOUT LOVING THE SELF, whether on the radio or in an interview for a magazine, at some point I am always asked the same question. With great earnestness, the presenter or journalist will ask: "But surely, if we love ourselves like you say, wouldn't we all become very selfish? What about *giving*?"

Stifling an inner groan, I remind them that one can only give if one has something to give. If you don't give to yourself first, how can you possibly give to others? You will be like a beggar, undernourished, demanding and desperate.

But their question is understandable. We have all been conditioned not to love ourselves, but to be there for other people (think about codependency). If we could really do this, perhaps it would not be too bad. The world might be a happier place, albeit at the expense of our own personal happiness. But our first job is to make ourselves happy. Whenever we do, our joy ripples out and affects our environment, which means not only other people, but, we are told by scientists, plants as well. We are all part of one Whole, and when we celebrate being alive, the whole of existence celebrates with us.

But it is hard to celebrate if you are afraid. And the world is full of fear. Paranoia is perhaps the biggest problem in the world today: fear of scarcity, that makes us hoarders and exploiters, competitive and greedy; fear of nations for each other, which is what is behind the frittering away of resources on so-called "defense;" fear of our fellow man that spills out in violence in our cities.

Never before in history have more people been more afraid, but then, never before has our planet been so threatened by ruptured ozone layers, pollution of our rivers and seas, the "greenhouse effect," and the ever-present possibility of annihilation by nuclear war.

And politicians have not been much help in allaying our disquiet. These so-called leaders are more concerned with increasing rather than dispelling our paranoia. They are only interested in their public image and vote-catching, fiddling while Rome burns. It is not by playing politics that our world will continue to survive.

A drastic transformation is the only thing that can save us from extinction. We need to transform our consciousness from tribal to global, to be more aware of our power to create heaven or hell here now, and to take responsibility for doing so. We need to be more sensitive, to feel the interconnectedness of all living things and our own interdependence. Above all, we need more *respect*, for each other, and for the plant and animal kingdoms too that help to sustain life.

Our mother the Earth is groaning. She is in pain, and needs all the support from us that she can get. We can no longer take for granted that she will nourish and sustain us: she has enough problems of her own. We have to do it ourselves.

The Aquarian Age

We have been told by astrologers that the world is passing out of the Piscean Age and into the Age of Aquarius. This means that all of us have to work on ourselves to become more conscious and to take responsibility for the energy we put out into the world. We can no longer rely on teachers and groups, or on the tribe. We are now on our own, for better or for worse.

More and more of us are doing this already. We have seen the danger signals, and the more reflective among us are disquieted by what we see. So we may be contributing to organizations like Greenpeace or Amnesty International, or responding to appeals for support for the vast numbers of our fellow men, women and children who are in desperate need all over the world. And this is good.

But it is not enough. Nothing less will do than the total transformation of *ourselves*, of the evolution of a new consciousness in us all which would make violence, whether to our fellows or to our beautiful blue planet, unthinkable.

But how is this New Age Consciousness to come about? The answer is by taking responsibility, by patiently working on ourselves, to become more aware, more loving. The rest will follow naturally. It will spread. As Lao Tzu put it: "Love the world as your own self; then you can truly care for all things" (*Tao Te Ching, 13*).

It must make God weep to see the horrible things that are carried on in His name today, in the name of religion, that was meant to be the Light of the World. Instead, it has in some places plunged the world into even worse darkness, for the perversion of the best is always the worst.

"Be a light unto yourself"

Buddha's last words to his brother Anand before he died were, "Be a light unto yourself." His whole system was based on the quest for Enlightenment, which simply means knowing who you are and living it. And knowing who we really are means to realize our divinity—and everybody else's—our relationship to the Whole, and that this is our home.

There is the story of the guest who was invited to a christening. She turned out in reality to be a wicked witch who whispered into the infant's ear: "You are special." The moral of the story has always been that as a result we are all trying desperately to live up to what she told us.

But in fact, that old witch knew a thing or two. For

the truth is that we *are* special. Either we all are—or nobody is. We are all, every single one of us, unique, special, amazing and *magnificent*. And that includes YOU.

Love, peace and joy.

Further Reading

Creating Abundance Andrew Ferguson (Piatkus Books)

Creative Visualization Shakti Gawain (Bantam Books)

Codependency David Stafford and Liz Hodgkinson (Piatkus Books)

Dare to Connect Dr. Susan Jeffers (Piatkus Books)

Feel the Fear and Do It Anyway Dr. Susan Jeffers (Arrow)

Getting Well Again Carl and Stephanie Simonton (Bantam Books)

Living in the Light Shakti Gawain (Whatever Publishing)

Love, Medicine and Miracles Bernie Siegel (Century Hutchinson)

Love is Letting Go of Fear Gerald Jampolsky (Celestial Arts)

Meditation for Everybody Louis Proto (Penguin)
You Can Heal Your Body Louise Hay (Eden Grove)
You Can Heal Your Life Louise Hay (Eden Grove)

Index

A